Why Johnny Doesn't Behave

Twenty Tips and Measurable BIPs

Barbara D. Bateman
Annemieke Golly

IEP
RESOURCES

Authors: Barbara D. Bateman and Annemieke Golly
Editor: Tom Kinney
Graphic Design: Sherry Pribbenow

An Attainment Publication

©2003 Attainment Company, Inc. All Rights Reserved.
Printed in the United States of America

P.O. Box 930160
Verona, Wisconsin 53593-0160
Phone 800-651-0954   Fax 800.942.3865
www.AttainmentCompany.com
ISBN 1-57861-490-2

Barbara Bateman

Barbara Bateman, Ph.D., J.D. is a nationally recognized expert in special education and in special education law. She has taught special education students in public schools and institutions, conducted research in learning disabilities, assessment, visual impairments, mental retardation, attitudes toward people with disabilities, and effective instruction for children with disabilities. She joined the faculty of the special education department at the University of Oregon in 1966 and while there also held visiting or summer appointments at several universities including the University of Virginia, the University of Maine, and the University of Wisconsin. She has authored over 100 professional articles, monographs, chapters and books. Dr. Bateman graduated from the University of Oregon School of Law in 1976, the year before the federal special education law (then called P.L. 94-142 and now known as IDEA) went into effect, and since then has worked in all 50 states, serving as a hearing officer, an expert witness, a consultant to attorneys and agencies, a speaker, and a teacher of special education law. Presently, Dr. Bateman is a special education consultant in private practice. When not writing, conducting in-service education for school districts, providing assistance to parents of children with disabilities, consulting with attorneys involved in IDEA legal actions, Dr. Bateman can be found traveling the world with binoculars and snorkel in search of birds, fish and shells.

Annemieke Golly

Dr. Golly is a certified special education teacher and has taught children with behavior and conduct disorders for the past 25 years. Dr. Golly received her Ph.D., in special education at the University of Oregon. Her areas of expertise are preventive interventions, behavior management, classroom and school-wide management. She is currently working at the Institute on Violence and Destructive Behavior at the University of Oregon as a teacher trainer and program director for a four year legislative grant designed to implement the **First Step to Success Program: Early Intervention for Children with Challenging Behaviors**, state-wide in kindergarten classrooms. She is also program director for a recently awarded grant to adapt and implement the **First Step to Success** program for Headstart.

Dr. Golly has been a coordinator for designing and implementing an early intervention program, **First Step to Success**, for the past 10 years. She trained hundreds of teachers and coaches to implement school and home interventions for students with challenging behaviors.

Dr. Golly recently developed an early intervention program for pre-school students with challenging behaviors: **First Step to Success, preschool version**. In the past year, she coauthored a training manual for **Effective School and Classroom Management K–12**. She has worked as a consultant/trainer to implement behavior management strategies in the United States, Canada, The Virgin Islands, Germany and South Africa. She has taught numerous university courses and school district teacher and parent training courses.

Annemieke was born and raised in Veghel, The Netherlands. She was one of six children and had to leave school at age 15 to work with her dad as a mechanic and secretary in the family car business. She eventually married an American Air force officer and moved to the United States. They had two children four years apart, Mark and Ivette. When son Mark started school in Eugene, Oregon, he was diagnosed with minimal brain damage and they were told that Mark would probably never learn to read or write. Dr. Barbara Bateman advised Annemieke to seek help from Sigfried

Engelmann, the author of a Direct Instruction Program: DISTAR. Zig Engelmann taught Annemieke how to teach her son Mark and within 3 months, Mark had mastered the entire first grade and part of the second grade curriculum in reading. Mark eventually graduated from college with a BA in business. Annemieke proceeded to voluntarily teach reading at Spangdalhem Air force Base for four years to students grades one through six. She returned to Eugene, Oregon to become an instructional assistant in an elementary school. Annemieke obtained her GED at age 38 and took classes at the local community college. She eventually transferred to the University of Oregon where she received her BA, Masters and Ph.D. degrees. Her claim to fame is that she has never failed to teach a child to read in the past 25 years.

Annemieke currently lives in Eugene, Oregon with her partner Dr. Michael Rebar. Her children, Mark and Ivette and her husband Scott Johnson live in Eugene as well.

Skilled teachers know that most potential behavior problems can be prevented altogether and many others 'nipped in the bud.' However, some students present behaviors so challenging that more structured interventions are required, usually across more settings than just the classroom. Often these students have been identified as needing special education or related services such as counseling.

In this book, we first present Twenty Tips for teachers which will minimize and greatly reduce student problem behaviors and increase positive social interactions. Secondly, we discuss functional behavioral analyses (FBAs) and behavior intervention plans (BIPs) which are required when a teacher must deal with more extreme behaviors and with special education students whose behavior interferes with learning.

Developing Effective Positive Behavioral Intervention Plans

What is the single most important skill teachers need? When asked this question, regular education and special education teachers overwhelmingly reply **"management of behavior."** All else in the school and in the classroom depends on behavior management, and without it, little of value can be accomplished. As society's norms and expectations for student behavior have changed, behavior management has taken on new, increased importance. No longer do children say, "Yes, ma'am" and "No, sir," sit quietly when asked, or respond to adults with unfailing politeness and respect. Perhaps they never really did. Regardless, enjoyable and successful teaching requires a positive atmosphere and appropriate behavior in the classroom.

Experienced, skilled teachers know that many potential behavior problems can be prevented altogether and most others 'nipped in the bud.' However, some students present behaviors so challenging that more structured interventions are required, usually across more settings than just the classroom. Often these students have been identified as needing special education or related services such as counseling.

In this book, we first present Twenty Tips for teachers which will minimize and greatly reduce student problem behaviors and increase positive social interactions. These Twenty Tips are followed by structured behavioral analyses and intervention plans which are required when a teacher must deal with more extreme behaviors and with special education students whose behavior interferes with learning.

The principles of preventing inappropriate behaviors and teaching more appropriate replacement behaviors are the same for all students.

Challenging behaviors are presented by regular and special education students alike. The principles of preventing inappropriate behaviors and teaching more appropriate replacement behaviors are the same for all students. The process of assessing the effectiveness of our interventions is the same for all students and is dependent upon using measurable behavior goals. What is different for special education students is that the Individuals with Disabilities Education Act (IDEA) requires (a) that the IEP team consider strategies, including positive interventions, to deal with behavior that interferes with the special education student's own learning or that of others (34 CFR 300.346(a)(2)); (b) that before a disciplinary removal of a special education student from school for more than 10 days in a school year, the IEP team must review an existing behavioral intervention plan (BIP) or, if none exists, conduct a functional behavioral assessment (FBA) and implement a BIP based on that FBA (34 CFR 300.520(b)), and (c) that if a child who has a BIP and has been removed for more than 10 days is to be removed again (even for a one day suspension), the BIP must be reviewed and modified, if necessary (34 CFR 300.520(a)). These FBAs and BIPs must be committed to writing as documentary evidence that the school is in compliance with IDEA.

The keys to developing BIPs are thinking in objective measurable terms and making measurements upon which we can base educational decisions. These are the essential ingredients in improving student classroom behaviors. Changing behaviors may be more crucial to the success of some special education students than for some regular education students, but inappropriate behaviors, unchanged, can be the educational and post-school undoing of any student.

Measurability of behavioral goals and objectives is legally mandated only for students who have IEPs, but it is just as important for any student whose behaviors interfere with school success. Therefore, we strongly recommend that teachers use BIPs and FBAs as IDEA requires for special education students, with those whose behavior is of concern. The principles of changing behavior are the same for all of us. We will not distinguish between special education and regular education students except for an

> *The principles of changing behavior are the same for all of us. We will not distinguish between special education and regular education students except for an occasional reminder that certain practices are legally required only for special education students.*

Chapter	Regular Education	Special Education
I. Introduction		
II. Creating a Positive Classroom Environment for all Students	Best Practices	Best Practices
III. Developing FBAs and BIPs	Best practices; often necessary; not required by law	BIPs required by IDEA when behavior impedes learning of student or others; FBAs required in some disciplinary situations
IV. Measuring Behavioral Progress	Not required by law, but nevertheless essential	Mandatory by IDEA
V. Basic Plans and Final Words	Best Practices	Best Practices

Fig. 1 Behavioral Intervention with Special and Regular Education Students

occasional reminder that certain practices are legally required only for special education students. Nevertheless, they are just as helpful for all. Fig. 1 outlines each chapter and how it applies to regular and special education students.

All teaching and managing strategies offered in this book are efficient, effective and supported by research. Nearly every sentence could include one or more references to that research. We've chosen not to do that as our intent is to provide a practical guide for teachers and parents. We have included a few carefully selected references that will be helpful to the interested reader.

Chapter II

Creating a Positive Classroom Environment for all Students

Creating a Positive Classroom Environment for all Students

Students frequently misbehave because they (1) want and need attention from adults and peers, (2) are trying to avoid a difficult or unpleasant task (too difficult, too easy, too boring), or (3) for some older students, revenge. Additionally, students may misbehave due to undiagnosed conditions such as hearing or vision deficits, sleep deprivation, substance abuse or mental illness. It is imperative that medical conditions be attended to by appropriate support systems within the school (social worker, school nurse, counselor) or outside the school (psychologist, community resources). Whether or not their issues are being addressed, the teacher must continue to help students be as successful as possible academically and behaviorally. This can be a challenging task, but it is the task teachers are paid to perform.

> *Fortunately, most students are "low maintenance," and come to school eager to learn and socialize and do so with a minimum of teaching effort. However, each classroom usually has a few students who are high maintenance.*

Fortunately, most students are "low maintenance," and come to school eager to learn and socialize and do so with a minimum of teaching effort. They learn in spite of poor classroom management and teaching skills. However, each classroom usually has a few students who are high maintenance. They require an enormous amount of teacher time, patience and resources. When schools encounter these students, things must be in place throughout the school for the teacher to stay sane and for all students to have a successful year (Sprague, Golly, Bernstein, March, & Munkres, 1999). The following **Twenty Tips** help all students, but are essential for children with challenging behaviors to be successful in the classroom environment.

Establish clear expectations for the class.
√ **What do you want to hear?**
√ **What do you want to see?**

Expectations for student behaviors vary from adult to adult because we all have different tolerance levels. The adult in the classroom needs to know what is tolerable in her classroom in order to be effective and efficient when working with students. Having clear expectations and knowing which classroom behaviors are acceptable help create a positive and respectful environment for all students, especially those with challenging behaviors.

Students need to know what is expected when they arrive at school. Routines and procedures such as (a) taking care of personal items (coats, backpacks, homework), engaging in activities before class starts (go to desk, socialize, read books, play games), (c) asking for help appropriately (raise hand, display sign, line up at the teacher's desk), (d) dealing with personal needs (drinks, bathroom, seating), (e) being organized (pencil sharpening, obtaining paper, supplies, books), (f) making transitions (moving to different groups or classes, taking a break, eating lunch, ending the day), (g) engaging in buffer activities (entering the classroom, finishing an assignment) and (h) having lunch. In addition, students must know the acceptable noise level during different times of the day. They need to be taught when it's acceptable to talk and when it's not.

> *Having clear expectations and knowing which classroom behaviors are acceptable helps create a positive and respectful environment for all students, especially those with challenging behaviors.*

Once expectations are clear and have become an automatic part of their repertoire, students and teacher alike feel organized and calm and can focus on academic content and learning. But how does a teacher teach these vital routines and procedures?

Tip #
2

Directly teach expectations.
√ **Model and role-play using examples and non-examples.**
√ **Reinforce until automatic.**
√ **Use class-wide motivational systems.**
√ **Reinforce intermittently for maintenance.**
√ **Review and/or reteach when necessary.**

Clearly defined expectations alone are not sufficient. Adults too often assume that students know how to behave and perform in a safe, responsible and respectful manner. This assumption is erroneous. When a student doesn't perform according to clear rules and expectations, he needs to be taught explicitly how to do so. It is not helpful to assume a student knows how to behave but "chooses" not to.

Behavior skills and expectations must be taught like academic skills (Walker, 1995). If a student constantly makes errors during long division because she has not mastered subtraction skills, the teacher patiently teaches subtraction until she is firm and can be successful at long division. However, if a student constantly breaks a rule (talking without raising hand), he is often scolded or removed from class without additional teaching. The student is somehow expected to return to class knowing how to perform the hand raising skill, without it having been taught.

When a student doesn't perform according to clear rules and expectations, he needs to be taught explicitly how to do so. It is not helpful to assume a student knows how to behave but "chooses" not to.

Modeling with role-play is an effective way to teach behavioral expectations. First, the teacher models the skill and shows, *"This is the right way. This is not the right way."* Next, the teacher pretends to be the student and the students pretend to be the teacher. The teacher acts out a routine, like hand raising, and asks the students whether she performed it correctly. Next, she demonstrates a non-example (i.e., does the routine incorrectly) and asks for feedback. This procedure is repeated several times ending with a positive example of the skill.

Acting the behavior out is more effective than telling students what they should or shouldn't do. Demonstration and role-play are effective for all students, especially younger students and children with attention, language and cognitive deficits. Props can be used to provide effective, unambiguous nonverbal feedback that doesn't interrupt the role play. Such props can be used across all settings. A card that is

If a student constantly breaks a rule (talking without raising hand), he is often scolded or removed from class without additional teaching. The student is somehow expected to return to class knowing how to perform the hand raising skill, without it ever having been taught.

red on one side and green on the other side can be used as an effective role-play prop. Green means, *"Go. That's the right way. Keep doing what you are doing"* and red means, *"Stop. Do not keep doing what you are doing. Change to doing the right thing."* While the teacher pretends to be a student, students can provide him with immediate feedback by turning the card to the appropriate color. He can provide the students with positive feedback such as, *"Wow, you are excellent teachers. You know exactly when I do it the right way and when I don't do it the right way."* Students like to be in control and provide the teacher with feedback.

The card can also be used by the teacher to provide feedback to the entire class when practicing a skill like hand raising. For example, provide a motivational chart (rocket, thermometer, baseballs, cars) with several spaces to be filled. The class earns points for keeping the card on green for a period of time, earning a filled space on the chart at the end of the session. When all spaces are filled, the class earns a special activity (free time, board games, special story). The motivational system and language used must be age appropriate.

When a new skill is firm and students consistently perform it, another skill (e.g., following directions the first time they are given) is targeted. Every once in a while, remind students how well they are doing on a previously mastered skill. Say, *"May I have your attention please. I just want you to know that I've noticed how respectful you have been this past week by consistently raising your hand when you have something to say."*

If at some point students fall back into old habits and make errors again, reteach the skill and reinforce its correct performance. Provide students with more frequent positive feedback in the beginning and slowly fade as the skill becomes firm.

Tip # 3

Pay attention to the behavior you want.

√ Teach: *"You never know when you will get a surprise."*

√ Notice which behavior, appropriate or inappropriate, gets more attention.

The teacher needs to know the individual goals on which students are working so they can provide positive feedback for efforts toward reaching them. For example, one goal may be to use appropriate language in class. After having taught the expectations through examples and non-examples when the student has used appropriate language during part of a period, say, "May I have your attention please? You never know when you will get a surprise. John, I noticed that you have been respectful ever since we started class. Your language has been very appropriate. Here is a ticket for 10 minutes of free time, computer time, or a soda." Keep track of who receives the surprise so that during the course of a week all students get noticed for something they have done well. When a goal is reached, focus on refining another behavior. Even when all students are consistently following classroom expectations, stop once in a while and let them know by saying something like, "May I have your attention please? I want you to know how respectful and responsible all of you are. You

The teacher who falls into the "criticism trap" and constantly notices students "not doing the right thing," faces more behavior problems than do teachers who provide positive feedback for correct behaviors. This does not mean, however, that all inappropriate behavior should be ignored.

have been working so well all morning, I would like to surprise you by (reading favorite poem, turning on music, going out for extra break, having a snack, playing board games)."

The more attention you pay to the behavior you want from students, the more it will happen. They will be more likely to work respectfully and responsibly in the future because they know you will notice. The teacher who falls into the "criticism trap" and constantly notices students "not doing the right thing," faces more behavior problems than do teachers who provide positive feedback for correct behaviors. This does not mean, however, that all inappropriate behavior should be ignored.

Minimize attention for minor inappropriate behavior.

√ Use only a few words if the problem is small.
√ Don't make a mountain out of a molehill.

If a student is acting inappropriately to obtain teacher attention (talking out in class, getting out of seat), the teacher may choose to ignore that behavior and provide positive feedback to students following directions. As soon as the offending student is doing the right thing, the teacher may approach the student and say something like, "You made a good choice to sit down and do your work." Be proactive and catch the student doing the right thing before misbehavior occurs.

If the teacher feels the need to say something about inappropriate behavior, the statement should be short and neutral in tone. For example, "That's not okay. You need to sit down and open your book to page 5." Immediately provide positive feedback to students who are doing the right thing: "John, I see that you have your book open to page 5.

If the teacher feels the need to say something about inappropriate behavior, the statement should be short and neutral in tone.

Sally, you have started on the problems on page 5." As soon as the target student is complying, provide reassuring feedback, "Good choice following directions. Let me know if you need help."

A teacher should not ignore inappropriate behavior that involves more than one student or that is hurting someone. Rather than escalating the situation by trying to figure out what is going on, provide short, clear directions for what the students need to be doing. For example, *"John, go to your desk and work on the puzzle. Len, get the book about Ping from my desk, go to your table and look at the book for a few minutes."*

Tip #
5

Give short and clear directions.
√ Use alpha, not beta commands.
√ Tell students what to do instead of what not to do.

Short and clear directions can be referred to as alpha commands. Commands that are wordy, long and convey teacher frustrations are called beta commands (Walker & Walker, 1991). Alpha commands are far more effective, especially when dealing with students who have attention deficit, oppositional defiance or conduct disorders, or are seriously emotionally disturbed. These students are often frustrating to deal with, and it takes a skilled teacher to help them be successful. The teacher must refrain from lecturing them and inadvertently increasing their guilt feelings. Often these students attend only to the first few words said. Furthermore, lengthy or frustrated commands provide the wrong model for the other students who then think that it is okay to talk down to these students. These students will be more disliked by their peers when they are seen as being disliked by the teacher. These students are often tattled on because their

Students will be more disliked by their peers when they are seen as being disliked by the teacher. These students are often tattled on because their peers think the teacher wants to hear negative things about them.

peers think that the teacher wants to hear negative things about them.

When students are misbehaving, teachers must remember to give clear and concise directions about what students need to be doing, not what they shouldn't be doing. Say something like, *"Pick up your chair, sit down and draw a picture of your dog,"* instead of, *"How many times have I told you not to get up out of your seat? Don't you know how to act in this class? I've told you what to do a hundred times. Now, get to work."* This beta command does not give the student specific information on what needs to be done. It also conveys signs of frustration from the teacher.

Tip #
6

Use an attention signal.

√ **Teach students to stop what they are doing and focus on you.**

√ **Use the signal as a preventive too.**

Most teachers have a way to get students to listen to them — a bell, xylophone, or rhythmic clapping. The problem is that students stop for a moment and go right back to what they were doing, instead of listening to the teacher. Students need to be explicitly taught that, *"When I ring the bell and ask for your attention, you are to stop what you are doing, put your eyes on me and listen until I tell you to go back to work again."* This strategy is effective for people of all ages. Listening when someone is talking is an important skill to have and one which conveys respect. Failure to listen conveys disrespect.

This strategy for gaining student attention also can be used as a preventive interaction. For example, a group of students are getting involved in an activity and start laughing and roughhousing. If this behavior continues, it may escalate into a fight. Instead of approaching the students and telling them to get their act together, give the usual audible signal and say, *"May I have your attention please?"* After all students are standing quietly, say, *"Thank you for giving me your attention right away.*

Are there any questions about the assignment? I will come around and see how everyone is doing. I need you to work quietly and respectfully in your groups."
The teacher did not single out the small group for a reprimand. The entire class was asked to listen. This strategy provides the problem students a moment to calm down and reassures the rest of the class that the teacher will monitor class behavior.

Tip # 7

Define clear consequences for unacceptable behavior.

√ **Know what is not tolerable in your classroom.**

√ **Know what steps you will take when unacceptable behavior occurs.**

Even if the teacher has done all the preventive interactions mentioned above, some students will need a negative consequence to change their behavior. Discuss with them what is not acceptable in your classroom. Depending on the age of the students, it can be helpful to let them brainstorm ideas about what behaviors are not acceptable. However, keep the discussion about inappropriate behavior controlled. If students offer extreme ideas, minimize attention for the inappropriate comment and simply say, *"That's not appropriate. Who can give me another idea?"*

The teacher must be very clear about the bottom line for unacceptable behavior. Most schools have defined zero tolerance behaviors and consequences for bringing weapons, but the teacher also needs to know how to follow through on every other classroom behavior that is not tolerable such as violence, chronic disrespect and destruction of property. The teacher may use time-out, office referrals, loss of privileges, restitution or contact with parents. The teacher must have a continuum of actions clearly defined for unacceptable behavior. As the teacher gets to know each student, consequences may vary

> *Even if the teacher has done all the preventive interactions we have mentioned, some students will need a negative consequence to change their behavior.*

among them. What may be punishing to one student may not be punishing to another student. If the behavior does not change after the "punishment," it's safe to assume the consequence was not punishing enough.

Tip #8

Teach consequences for unacceptable behavior.

√ **Inform students of possible consequences.**
√ **The time-out procedure must be taught before it is used.**

As with all behavior expectations, the consequences for unacceptable behavior need to be explicitly taught. If the teacher has decided that taking a time-out or being sent to the principal's office are the consequences, students must be taught what it looks like to follow them. It is advisable to role-play these scenarios with another adult. The teacher may say something like, *"I know that all of you are going to do your best to follow directions and be responsible, respectful and safe in this classroom. Sometimes one of you may make a mistake and I will ask you to go to time-out. This is what I expect you to do. You walk to the small room in back of the class. As soon as you sit quietly in the blue chair, I will start the timer and set it for three minutes. When the timer rings and you have been quiet, you may come back and join the group. I will not talk to you while you are in time-out. If you decide to be disrespectful by screaming, kicking or bothering others, you may lose the privilege to be in time out, and I will decide what other special privileges (going to lunch or recess on time, computer time, movie, going home on time) you will lose. You will also need to make up the time you lost when you were being uncooperative by doing a time-out."* After the explanation, the two adults can role-play examples and non-examples of going to time-out. For older students, a trip to the office, phone call to the parent, or detention

> *As with all behavior expectations, the consequences for unacceptable behavior need to be explicitly taught.*

may be more appropriate consequences. The most important principle here is that teachers and students understand the expectations and consequences so they do not have to figure them out during a crisis. In some cases, teachers may use self-created videotapes to show students examples and non-examples of acceptable behaviors. Again, being proactive is more effective than being reactive and having to make discipline decisions on the spot when they have not been carefully preplanned.

Tip # *9*

If unacceptable student behavior does not change, the teacher's behavior must change.

√ **Determine what makes the misbehavior effective for the student.**

√ **When the behavior doesn't change, what you are doing is not working.**

The teacher must monitor whether consequences are effective. If the teacher has to punish a student for the same behavior over and over, the punishment is not working and the teacher needs to do something else. For example, a student is sent to the principal's office for throwing and tearing up books in the classroom. If in the next few days, this behavior occurs repeatedly, and each time the teacher applies the same consequence with the same lack of result, it's safe to assume that being sent to the office is not effective. This student may like to be sent to the office for a number of unknown reasons. There may be something going on in the classroom that he wants to avoid (assignment, peer pressure, environmental issues such as temperature), or perhaps he likes the attention (teacher scolding, principal discussing, peers watching). One way to find out what is going on is to turn the scenario around and allow the student to earn time with the principal for appropriate behavior. The teacher could say, *"It seems like you are having a difficult time being respectful during science class. How about this . . . tomorrow, if you show respect for the first 45 minutes by following directions, keeping your book on your desk and speaking appropriately, you can earn the privilege of going to the office and talking to the principal about (your favorite TV program, hobby or interest).*" If the behavior changes, going to the office could be earned through longer and longer periods of following directions and being respectful. Eventually it could become a routine privilege.

The process of determining if the misbehavior was getting something the student wanted or was avoiding something he didn't want is called functional behavioral assessment or analysis (FBA). More will be said later about FBAs.

Tip #
10

Inappropriate behavior is an effective and efficient way to get attention.
√ **Doing the right thing often goes unnoticed.**
√ **Being inappropriate is a sure way to get attention.**

If a well-behaved student is in a classroom with 25 or more children, it's unlikely she receives a lot of individual attention from the teacher. Most of the teacher's attention is directed toward students with challenging behaviors. Luckily, many well-behaved students require little individual teacher attention as they get reinforcement from learning and completing required tasks, as well as from peers and adults around them. On the other hand, a student who needs a lot of attention, who has an attention deficit (i.e., does not receive as much as he needs), discovers quickly that doing the right thing often goes unnoticed. This student will have learned early in her school career that inappropriate behavior receives immediate attention. The result of inappropriate behavior is predictable and effective for the student. If one uses inappropriate language, throws a tantrum, destroys property or hurts someone, it can be guaranteed that the teacher will say or do something immediately. Therefore, the teacher

A student who needs a lot of attention discovers quickly that doing the right thing often goes unnoticed.

This student will have learned early in his school career that inappropriate behavior receives immediate attention.

must give this child a great deal of attention for appropriate behavior before inappropriate behavior — which **must** be responded to — can occur. Remember, attention from adults and peers is guaranteed when inappropriate behavior occurs. It is predictable. The teacher must prevent its occurrence.

Tip #
11

Always treat the student with respect.
√ **Stay calm.**
√ **Use a neutral tone.**

The saying, "Do as I say, not as I do," probably was invented because — while parents and teachers preach about good behaviors — children nonetheless imitate them by arguing, using inappropriate language, fighting and saying negative things about others. From an early age, children imitate the actions of others around them[1]. If a student is not liked by other students or the teacher, there is little hope she will do well in school. Sadly, children who are rejected by peers at an early age are at a higher risk for juvenile delinquency than popular students. Therefore, it is extremely important that all students are treated with respect. Adults must model respectful interactions because children will "Do as you do."

> *If a student is not liked by other students or the teacher, there is little hope she will do well in school. Sadly, children who are rejected by peers at an early age are at a higher risk for juvenile delinquency than popular students. Therefore, it is extremely important that all students are treated with respect.*

One of the most important teacher skills is the ability to stay calm. Even when a student is trying to "push your buttons," remain in control. Give the student a short, clear direction in a neutral tone and walk away calmly. Standing over a student, shaking a finger, or raising your voice are not respectful actions. Belittling a student or using sarcasm are unacceptable and inappropriate reactions to any kind of behavior. Suppose Johnny

---

[1]When a child does not imitate, learning is impaired. Many children who have autism do not imitate.

repeatedly ignores the signal to stop working when time is up. One day, the behavior becomes intolerable. The teacher walks up to Johnny, hands on hips, gives a big sigh and in front of the entire class says something like: *"How many times have I told you? When the bell rings, you need to stop and get ready for lunch. Every day I*

> *Belittling a student or using sarcasm are unacceptable and inappropriate reactions to any kind of behavior.*

have to tell you over and over again to follow directions. I'm sick and tired of having to remind you all the time. Look at the rest of the class. They all did it right away . . ." and on and on. This type of teacher behavior is unacceptable. Not only does it give undivided attention to inappropriate behavior, but it shows the rest of the class it's okay to talk down to Johnny. In addition, the class sees Johnny causing grief to the teacher, and will take it out on him during recess or other unstructured times. They will tattle on him even if he is absent because they think the teacher wants to hear bad things about him. Even if Johnny's behavior is annoying, it's the teacher's job to show respect and minimize attention for inappropriate behavior. In the above scenario, the teacher simply says in a neutral tone, *"Johnny, when the bell rings, you need to clean up. I noticed that the students at the table in the back started to clean up right away. I see that the people over here are getting ready for lunch quickly."* In addition, the teacher needs to find positive things about Johnny and point them out to the class to show he is as respected as the rest of the students. For example, it's time for reading and the teacher has asked students to open their books to page 5. The teacher is standing next to Johnny. As soon as Johnny opens his book the teacher says, *"May I have your attention please. I want you to notice that Johnny followed directions right away by opening his book to page 5. As soon as everyone is at the right spot, we can start. Thank you, Johnny."* For every negative comment the child receives, there should be at least five positive ones to preserve his self-esteem. Students with annoying behaviors can be very frustrating. However, teachers must remember that it is their job to try to make all students as successful as possible. If most of the points discussed above are in place and there are still times a student is not doing well, try humor.

Tip #
12

Use humor, never sarcasm.
√ **Keep things light; it's not the end of the world.**
√ **Sarcasm can be worse than spanking.**

Students don't usually misbehave because they purposely want to upset the teacher. Misbehavior generally happens because of an unmet need such as attention; avoiding a task that is too difficult or too easy, needing power and control, feeling insecure or the need to feel like a person who belongs. Sometimes it looks like a student is defiant and oppositional, but she may simply not know what needs to be done at that moment. Give the student the benefit of the doubt and keep your initial interactions light. For example, suppose Annie is working on the computer (she is not being tested), and she hesitates when asked to pull down the menu — a skill she performs on a daily basis. Don't automatically assume she is being defiant. She

> *Students have other issues going on in their lives, and school should be a safe place where they can count on adults to work with them without playing mind games or instilling guilt feelings.*

may be nervous about the request and confused for a moment. Instead of making a sarcastic remark like, *"Don't tell me you don't know where the menu is; you have only used it a million times!,"* say something like, *"Sometimes when I hear the word menu, it makes me think of food. The menu is right there on the top left hand side."* If this issue surfaces repeatedly, Annie needs to be pre-corrected and set up for success on future tries. Students have other issues going on in their lives, and school should be a safe place where they can count on adults to work with them without playing mind games or instilling guilt feelings. Remembering that most situations are not "the end of the world" fosters positive student teacher relations.

One trap adults fall into with students is getting into power struggles. This occurs when the adult asks the child to do something and he refuses. The adult insists he should do what was asked, and the child continues to refuse. Power struggles happen because the adult thinks, "When I ask a student to do something, he should do it," or "What will the other students think if I let this student get away with this," or "This student needs to learn who is boss around here."

Avoid power struggles!
√ **Participating in power struggles leads to disrespect.**
√ **Teach students how to engage you appropriately.**

Tip #
13

Power struggles are no-win situations. The adult may eventually force the child to comply because he is bigger and stronger. All this teaches is that it's acceptable to force one's will onto someone who is not as strong. Also, if the adult forces the issue to save face in front of the other children, the child is humiliated, becomes more angry and may become a target for others.

Avoid power struggles at all costs.

Avoid power struggles at all costs. For example, after giving the request, "Open your book to page 5," walk away and wait 5 seconds. If the student is not complying, repeat the request in a calm, matter-of-fact voice, not looking the student in the eye or shaking fingers. Walk away and provide other students with positive feedback. If the student still doesn't comply but is not hurting others or self, start keeping track of the time. Eventually, — 20 or 30 minutes later — the student will start following directions. Note the time and let the student know that she is making a good choice. When the period is over, ask her to wait for a moment. When all other

If the student is not complying, repeat the request in a calm, matter-of-fact voice, not looking the student in the eye or shaking fingers.

students have left, say, *"You made a good choice following directions during the last part of the period. What you did earlier was not okay. You will need to make up the wasted time during ...(recess, lunch time, preferred activity), and you must complete the work you missed."* This way, the student receives a consequence for inappropriate behavior, but it is dealt with in a respectful way.

If the student is trying to engage in power struggles to obtain attention, discuss privately how the student can get attention for appropriate behavior. For example, *"Charlie, you are so awesome at (drawing, singing, skateboarding, whistling, juggling)! If you show respect in class today, would you like to give a demonstration for the class?"*

Tip # 14

Get to know your students.

√ **Find ways to bond with each student.**

√ **Provide opportunities for students to talk to you.**

The relationship built between student and teacher when things are going well, can be very important when things don't go so well. While it's difficult for teachers with large numbers of students to connect with everyone, start by referring to them by first names, to give a sense of importance and belonging. Small, caring gestures such as a smile, a wink, a thumbs up or a touch on the shoulder can make a student feel special.

School personnel sometimes assume they know what is going on with a student before they have taken the time to talk to her. For example, a 16 year-old high school student, Barb, held a part time job, and had gone largely unnoticed during her school career. Suddenly, she started to miss classes, failed to turn in assignments, and her grades dropped

The relationship built between student and teacher when things are going well, can be very important when things don't go so well.

significantly. When Barb's teachers and school counselor met, they assumed that she was using drugs and needed to be taught a lesson. After further examination, the staff found out that her behavior was due to something very different. Her low income, single, working

> *Teachers are expected to do so many things that the essential task of helping students be behaviorally successful sometimes gets short shrift.*

mother had been taking care of Barb's sick grandmother who lived nearby. When Barb's mom was diagnosed with cancer and had to quit her job, Barb had to get an additional job to help the family, and had to take care of both her grandmother and her mom. As a result, her school performance dropped. Once the real facts were known and the staff became aware of Barb's situation, support was provided to lighten the burden for Barb and her family.

Teachers are expected to do so many things that the essential task of helping students be successful behaviorally sometimes gets short shrift. The teacher is the most important and powerful adult in a child's life next to parents or caregivers, an immediate and primary role model. Students want to be noticed by teachers as well as parents. Therefore, they should have opportunities to talk informally with you, one on one. These opportunities can be created by being around during unstructured times such as recess, lunch time, before and after school and on field trips. Give them a chance to spend a few minutes of personal attention. Structure it so the entire class has an opportunity to earn special recess, eating lunch in the room or outside, having a special picnic on the play field

> *Students want to be noticed by teachers. They should have opportunities to talk informally with you, one on one. These opportunities can be created by being around during unstructured times such as recess, lunch time, before and after school and on field trips.*

(as a classroom motivational system or "surprise") when no other classes are outside. During these times, the teacher has opportunities to interact one on one with several students. Casual information can be shared about home, friends and school. If the teacher wants to pursue the information she can say, *"Don, I would like it if you could have lunch with me in the classroom next Tuesday. We could have a chance to talk some more. What do you think?"* Have a specified time available once a week when students can sign up for a 10 minute private conference. Another way to communicate privately is a two-way journal between teacher and student. Many students will not need private time, but for those who do, the opportunity must be made. Students must feel they are an integral part of the school and feel they can openly to talk to the teacher or other adults in the school.

Create a safe environment for students.

√ **Practice controlling your emotional state.**
√ **Be a solid support.**

Creating a safe environment for students does not simply mean keeping weapons and intruders out of the school. A feeling of emotional safety is essential, especially for students who come from unstable and chaotic home environments. These students need predictability. They want the teacher to be their "rock," the person they can count on to help solve problems, to be empathic, to care and to offer emotional and physical support. They need a teacher who is respectful, fair and positive. Supportive adults are one of the main reasons many students like to go to school.

A feeling of emotional safety is essential, especially for students who come from unstable and chaotic home environments.

If students feel belittled, criticized or scolded by school staff, they will avoid going to school and may eventually drop out.

Tip # 16

Predictability is the key.

√ **Be structured.**

√ **Knowing what to expect provides opportunities to make choices.**

Being predictable means being structured. It can be seen as a rhythm. There must be a certain calming rhythm in the classroom. Routines such as how to enter the room, where to hang coats and put homework, attendance, lunch choices, breaks, group times, ending school, and the teacher's voice and smile are very comforting. If the teacher and students get into a rhythm and don't have to spend a lot of time deciding how to deal with everyday situations, they are more able to

When the school environment is predictable, it's easier for students to make choices.

spend valuable time learning important academic and social skills. When the school environment is predictable, it's easier for students to make choices. They can do it the right way and feel positive about being a group member, or they can receive a predictable consequence.

Collaborate with colleagues.

√ **Find an opportunity to share successes.**
√ **Drop into each other's classrooms.**

Being responsible for a group of students takes a great deal of effort and can be very lonely at times. When the responsibility and effort are shared with other adults, it can make a world of difference. It's rewarding to share successes with other staff members. Sharing new ideas, such as a different way to teach writing, an innovative science project, or the simple fact that your class came in after recess without incident is very reinforcing for the teacher. This can be done before a staff meeting, during grade level or department meetings, or via a list serve on e-mail.

> *Being responsible for a group of students takes a great deal of effort and can be very lonely at times. When the responsibility and effort are shared with other adults, it can make a world of difference. Seek out a staff member with whom to exchange quick and informal classroom visits.*

Another effective way to provide reinforcement for colleagues is to seek out a staff member with whom to exchange quick and informal classroom visits. Drop into another teacher's classroom unannounced and reinforce a specific, positive aspect of her classroom. For example, Ms. Jones' class has been working on a social studies unit on China. Mr. Lee walks into the class on his way to the office and says something like, *"Excuse me. Ms. Jones, I just wanted to stop by and see some of the pictures your students have made of the Great Wall."* Another example is to ask the playground or lunchroom supervisor to tell the teacher when the class or individual students have shown respect and responsibility during those unstructured times. Teachers too often hear only when things have not gone well.

They also need to hear when things do go well. Teachers as well as parents like hearing positive things about students.

Tip #
18

Work together with parents and caregivers.

√ **Make parents your allies, not your enemies.**

√ **Share more positives than negatives.**

When dealing with students who display challenging behaviors, remember that parents have had to deal with Johnny many hours a day for many years. Teachers often blame parents for unacceptable student behaviors, while parents often blame teachers for not giving their child needed help. Yet both parties want the best for the child. Parents, even ineffective ones, want their child to do well in school. Few, if any, parents say, *"I don't want Johnny to be successful in school."* Few, if any, teachers say, *"I don't want Johnny to be successful in school."* The common goal of parents and teachers is to help children be as successful as possible. Having parents as cooperative partners is very beneficial to a child's progress. A lack of effective communication too often causes a lack of cooperation between parents and teachers. Inviting parents into the classroom, making positive phone calls, e-mail messages and notes before problems occur establishes positive communication. When parents need to get involved because of a problem, it's much easier when good communication has already been established. Inviting them to school assemblies and activities when students perform is another way to encourage parents to become involved in a positive way.

> *Teachers often blame parents for unacceptable student behaviors, while parents often blame teachers for not giving their child needed help. Yet both parties want the best for the child. Parents, even ineffective ones, want their child to do well in school.*

In order for teachers to be effective with students, they need to take care of themselves. Different teachers have different needs. Some feel great if they exercise before they get to school in the morning. Others need a latte or a food item at a favorite stop before starting school. Some teachers prepare materials in the afternoon to be ready for the next day. Others do it early in the morning before classes start. Being organized also helps prevent behavior problems and creates a comfortable setting. Many behavior problems occur when materials are not ready, when students move from one activity to another, or when the teacher takes time to make copies or get books when class should have started.

Take care of your own needs, too.

√ **Organize and decorate the classroom for your comfort.**

√ **Don't be too hard on yourself.**

A typical teacher spends most of the day in one classroom, making it important that it be a comfortable and pleasant place to work. Create a classroom atmosphere according to your needs by arranging furniture, adding plants, pets, thematic bulletin boards, special places for showing off student work, announcements and so on. Try to make your classroom as low maintenance as possible by teaching students to keep it clean and organized and by having thematic bulletin boards that can stay-up for long periods of time. Simplify, simplify, simplify so you can teach, teach, teach!

A typical teacher spends most of the day in one classroom, making it important that it be a comfortable and pleasant place to work.

Tip #
20

Have passion and fun in your work.

√ **Remind yourself of the difference you can make.**

√ **Enjoy the special moments.**

The teacher's job is to help students be as successful as possible academically and socially. You are incredibly powerful and can make a huge difference in the lives of students positively, or negatively. It is the teacher who decides what the classroom standard and atmosphere will be. The teacher is in control of the classroom and teaches through modeling respect and problem solving. It's the teacher who needs to change his behavior and interact differently when things do not go well, so that students will change. Remember how important the job is and that it takes skill and passion to do it well. If you are doing the job just for the money, or find yourself constantly complaining about the students, it may be time to examine whether or not teaching is the right job for you. Teaching should be exciting and fun. Students are amazing and can be wonderfully creative in many ways. Relax and enjoy the special moments while helping to make students as successful as possible academically as well as socially!

Chapter III

Functional Behavior Assessments & Behavioral Intervention Plans

Functional Behavior Assessments and Behavioral Intervention Plans

Even when a superb teacher has implemented the Twenty Tips as well as humanly possible, trouble can loom. A student may transfer into the classroom from a punishing, chaotic environment. A devastating tragedy may befall a previously well-behaved student. A special education student's individualized education program (IEP) may be revised, leading the team to realize that certain behaviors require immediate intervention. Perhaps the student with challenging behaviors is newly identified as a special education student, and is now legally entitled to a behavior intervention plan (BIP). Something more than prevention is needed. It's time to intervene specifically to change behavior. First, examine the circumstances around the behavior and formulate a hypothesis as to what function the behavior is serving for the child. Then, develop a plan to change the behavior by changing what happens before and after that behavior typically occurs. This is what is meant by conducting a functional behavioral assessment (FBA) and developing a behavioral intervention plan (BIP).

Functional Behavioral Assessments (FBAs)

As indicated in the Introduction, the Individuals with Disabilities Education Act (IDEA) requires that when the behavior of a special education student impedes his learning or the learning of others, the IEP team must address that behavior and the strategies to deal with it, including positive interventions. Furthermore, this BIP must be reviewed and modified if a child's placement is to be changed. If a child is excluded from school for more than ten days for violating school rules, and does not have a BIP in place, then one must be developed, and it must be based on a FBA.

IDEA does not define the FBA required. Therefore, we look to accepted professional practice to establish what constitutes an appropriate FBA. First, understand that "functional" requires us to determine what function the target, undesirable behavior serves for the child. Typically, the child behaves inappropriately to get something he wants or to avoid something he doesn't want. An FBA allows us to determine what she is seeking or avoiding. Then we plan the interventions that teach appropriate ways to obtain desired results or to avoid them. The entire point of the FBA is to seek and obtain information needed to plan an effective behavioral intervention plan. It may be a simple, easy and quick analysis based on previous knowledge or records. On the other hand, it may require detailed observations or experimentation with various consequences.

At the heart of both the FBA and the BIP is the ABC sequence — **antecedent**, **behavior**, **consequence**. Something precedes the behavior (antecedent) and something follows it (consequence). In order to change a behavior, we must change the antecedent or the consequence or both. The FBA allows us to learn what significant antecedents or what consequences must be changed.

Antecedent	Behavior	Consequence
1. Teacher asks C to read aloud.	C hits another student.	C is sent to the office.
2. Wednesday mornings.	W falls asleep before recess.	W is sent to nurse's room.
3. Unstructured free time.	R draws lewd pictures.	Teacher takes R into workroom and talks to him about appropriate/inappropriate drawings.
4. Sixth grade teacher begins discussion in history.	M laughs, throws objects, whistles.	M stays in during recess.

ABC Examples

A common antecedent is that of a student being given work that is too difficult for him at his present performance level. Given this antecedent, he does whatever results in escape or avoidance. For example, some adults who have dyslexia recount the lengths to which they went to avoid reading in front of their peers. Almost no consequence a school could arrange is worse than the humiliation of having peers know how poorly they read. An extreme example of this was described in a psychologist's report of a sixth grader's reaction during testing of the boy's vocabulary. After the fourth time in a row that the student had to say he didn't know what a word meant, he had a catastrophic reaction:

> He was sitting in a folding chair in front of the couch. He shouted, "I am not stupid!" He held one arm up over his face and pushed his body back until the chair collapsed and he fell backward onto the couch. Those were the last words he said during that appointment. He pulled into a fetal ball and did not respond to any comfort, questions or other interventions. His Aunt, who was available in another part of the house, attempted to speak with him but to no avail. It was necessary to reschedule the assessment since he was clearly unable to continue.

> He is extremely sensitive to what he perceives as inadequacies, and when he was unable to answer the questions, he projected that others were thinking that he was stupid. He was extremely embarrassed, and angry at the same time. In this case, his response was to withdraw emotionally because he was unable to withdraw physically.[2]

In these situations, the antecedent (tasks beyond the present capability of the student) must be changed to prevent the inappropriate escape behaviors.

Sometimes, a consequence which the school intends to be a deterrent to the behavior (sending the student to library, study hall, office, nurse's room or another classroom) is more desirable to the student than the antecedent situation. A long time ago, in a tiny, rural school district, a seventh grade student was believed by her teacher to have said to another student that the teacher was a "fool." As punishment, she was sent into

---

[2]Used with permission of Dr. Georgia Carpenter.

the eighth grade classroom, which was taught by the principal, to spend a month. No "punishment" could have pleased the seventh grader more. The principal was a far better teacher and the curriculum more challenging and interesting, as perceived by the student. At the end of the month of "punishment," the seventh grader desperately sought escape back to the eighth grade room.

Sometimes a particular antecedent triggers an inappropriate behavior. For example, Marie skips school every Tuesday afternoon when she is scheduled to be in computer class. Assessment reveals that Marie is the only student in the class who has no computer at home, and the teacher expects that all students have access to one. Marie is unable, day after day, to complete her assigned homework, but is reluctant to reveal that her family has no computer. What must be changed is the antecedent, i.e., the combination of no access to a computer and the teacher's erroneous assumption that there *is* access.

Other times, the consequence which follows the behavior must be changed. For example, Jokin' John frequently interjects unexpected noises (squeaks, squawks, giggles, hiccups, belches, whistles) into classroom discussions and work periods. The other students laugh, snort, applaud and otherwise show their appreciation. That is what must be changed. The other children must be taught a different response, one which does not reinforce John.

An FBA — the examination of the pattern of antecedents, the target behavior, and the consequences — allows us to learn about the function of a given behavior for a given student and forms the firm foundation for a behavioral intervention plan. Without the FBA, there is a risk of serious error. Even with the FBA, we could be wrong about the function of the behavior. Our BIP is a test of the FBA hypothesis, and we must be prepared to re-analyze if our intervention is not quickly effective.

An FBA — the examination of the pattern of antecedents, the target behavior, and the consequences — allows us to learn about the function of a given behavior for a given student and forms the foundation for the BIP.

A real case illustrates this all too well. Vinny, (not his real name), a physically mature sixth grader, has been considered by his school to have the worst behavior problems ever seen in that part of the world. He has been expelled so often he has trouble remembering what grade he is in, and he has been referred to every juvenile authority possible.

An FBA was recently conducted by an independent evaluator who found exactly what many readers may have guessed — Vinny performs academically at a 2nd grade level and literally "freaks" out when confronted with 6th grade academic tasks he can't perform. Vinny has above average intelligence, but he has never been taught to perform academically at his true ability level or to cope appropriately when given tasks he cannot perform. Four years of extraordinary frustration for school personnel, family, and Vinny, might have been avoided had an FBA been conducted when his numerous and serious inappropriate behaviors began. Appropriate remedial teaching could have prevented years of negative experiences for all concerned. The frequency of students' misbehavior for the purpose (function) of avoiding "exposure" when school work is too difficult is hard to overestimate. For this reason, we offer the following case history of Dr. Golly's work with such a student:

> *The frequency of student misbehavior for the purpose (function) of avoiding "exposure" when school work is too difficult is hard to overestimate.*

Wes

I was asked to observe Wes, a fourth grader placed in a self-contained special education classroom for the past two years. The classroom consisted of a teacher, a full-time assistant, a practicum student and nine students ranging in ages from 9-12, seven boys and two girls. The classroom had a safe exclusionary time-out room, desks, computers and lots of toys as well as a door leading directly to the playground and another leading into the hallway across from the gymnasium.

Wes and his 13 year old brother had been adopted by their grandparents because their single mother was a serious drug user and could not take care of them. Wes did not show signs of aggression and non-compliance until the end of second grade. School staff told me he had been a friendly, kind and respectful student until then. At the end of second grade his inappropriate behavior had escalated to the point that he was identified as having a serious emotional disturbance and was put in his current placement, a self-contained special education classroom at his home school.

During his 2 years in the self-contained room, Wes had been placed in seclusionary time-out nearly every day. He was suspended from school at least 2 times a week (in spite of his IDEA eligibility and protections) for violent and verbally abusive behavior in the classroom and in the time-out room.

His grandparents were upset that Wes's behavior was not being dealt with at school and requested he not be sent home again. Searching for an alternative setting, the team proposed placing Wes in a day treatment center which would have been costly to the district. This is when I was asked to observe him.

When I got to the classroom, Wes was playing on a computer and was friendly and social. After about 20 minutes, the teacher asked all students to go to their seats for spelling. The teacher had a great positive reinforcement system to motivate the students and had written ten spelling words in cursive handwriting on the board and asked students to repeat the words after him. He handed out worksheets and instructed students to copy the words from the board. The worksheet had the same words printed on the bottom of the page.

The teacher instructed Wes to write just the first five words since they were at his level. Wes became extremely agitated and tore his page with a ruler and pencil. I walked over, touched the first word on the bottom of his page, read and circled it and put a small mark above it. I marked each of his five words and asked him to raise his hand as soon as he had finished copying them. He started right away and raised his hand promptly when he was finished. I told him that he had done an awesome job, and the teacher told me that this was the first time he had copied the words without blowing up.

I suspected that Wes couldn't read cursive writing. I asked the teacher about his reading level and was told he often refused to read. The teacher had tutored him for two years using a direct instruction program, Reading Mastery, the same one I had been using successfully for over twenty years. Wes ended up in time-out nearly each day for non-compliance.

When I observed the reading lesson, the teacher was not using the direct instruction reading manual, only the student reader. When I inquired about instruction, the teacher told me that he made up his own instruction while teaching Wes because he refused to work from the teacher manual. The teacher agreed to supply me with the appropriate direct instruction teacher manual the next day, so I could diagnose his reading deficiencies.

The following day, I brought a green/red card, a jar and lots of pennies. The teacher told me Wes was mechanically inclined and loved remote control trucks. I made a reinforcement system whereby he could earn pennies when the card was on green and the computer beeped at variable intervals. Wes could earn a dollar for each session. When he had earned 20 dollars, he would get a remote control truck. He was highly motivated.

I soon discovered he had mastered only six sounds and didn't know how to blend sounds. We worked for weeks. Wes was often non-compliant and verbally abusive. I would stay calm, restate the expectation and follow the reinforcement plan consistently. One day Wes became totally non-compliant and refused to work. I told him that he could tell me when he was ready to work. He sat with his arms crossed and fists folded saying things like, *"I'm not going to do the stupid work. You can't make me do this,"* and lots of obscene language. I ignored his comments and kept repeating the request, *"I will know that you are ready to work when you sit quietly and raise your hand."* I called the secretary on my cell phone and asked her to cancel all my appointments for the rest of the day. I called my family and told them I would probably be home very late that day and I would call later. I also made pretend calls and made-up conversations such as, *"Do you want me to write down all the fun ideas you have for students we work with who follow directions? Building rockets would be fun or having a Lego contest or a remote control car race.*" And so on. I also pretended to be doing work when I was not pretending to talk on the phone. After about 3 hours in the room, I called my partner Michael and asked him if he could bring my pajamas and overnight bag because I might be spending the night at school. Wes continued to be defiant and non-compliant. Several times he tried to run out of the room. I placed my chair in front of the door and sat there doing my pretend work. When he wanted my attention, I repeated my request calmly without giving him eye contact. I was determined to let him know that I was not going to let him get out of doing the task. After 5 hours, he raised his hand quietly and told me he was ready to work.

From that day on, he worked diligently, and after four months of tutoring for forty-five minutes a day, he was able to decode and read materials at third grade level. The following school year, he was placed in a resource room with 15 other children and a consistent direct instruction teacher who did not engage in power struggles. When Wes started to become non-compliant she would simply say, "You can choose to follow directions or go to time out until you're ready to read and make up the time after school. Wes timed himself out twice. He continued to make progress and ended up in fifth grade with minimal resource support.

Later, when I would visit his classroom, he proudly announced to his classmates that I was the best reading teacher in the world and that when I first met him he didn't know how to read. He would show me his fluency and accuracy charts and read a passage out of his latest book.

While learning the new skills, Wes ended up earning a remote control truck and a skateboard as motivators. The heavy reinforcement system was eventually faded out, and Wes worked to increase his fluency and accuracy. He graphed his accomplishments on a daily chart and proudly showed them to anyone interested in seeing them.

Wes has moved on to middle school where he is continuing to do well academically and behaviorally.

This true story illustrates two essential points. First, it shows the lengths to which a student will go to avoid something he experiences as painful. And second, it reveals how essential it is for the teacher to break the old, non-productive cycle, even if it takes five solid hours of intervention. Teachers must do what it takes, and an FBA helps us know just what it is that is required.

There is no such thing as **the** only way to do an FBA. In one situation, teachers and parents may be able to quickly, easily, and accurately identify antecedents, behaviors, and consequences, and thereby the "function" of the misbehavior. Other situations may require observations, interview, formal assessments, and more to pinpoint the antecedents and consequences of the target behavior. An FBA is adequate when it yields sufficient information to decide whether and how to modify antecedents consequences. Then it serves as the basis for developing a behavioral intervention plan.

The importance, legally and professionally, of doing an FBA when needed for a special education student is hard to overstate. Dussault (1998), a civil rights attorney, has cautioned school personnel in this regard:

"It would be a serious mistake for school districts to perceive that they only need to apply functional behavioral analysis and behavioral intervention plans to students who are currently subject to ongoing discipline systems. The law anticipates that the school district will have completed the functional behavioral analysis and behavioral intervention plan **before any behavior that results in disciplinary action arises** [emphasis added]. Unless the district uses FBA and BIPs with every child for whom behavior is a possible issue, the district may not be able to impose typical student discipline involving exclusion from a school program beyond the ten day period set forth in the Act [IDEA]. This is likely to include potentially all children who fall within the serious emotional disturbance category, the majority of children who are labeled autistic and brain injured, many children in the ADHD/LD categories and a significant number of children with other cognitive impairments . . .

The behavior must be dealt with in an affirmative **pro-active educational approach** [emphasis added] rather than through a reactive punitive approach[3]. (p. 148-163)"

Dussault goes on to caution against substituting a typical "behavior contract" (for the required FBA and BIP) which simply provides that if the student does certain behaviors, then specified negative consequences will occur. IDEA flatly requires the use of positive interventions. It is unlikely, according to Dussault, that a school could defend disciplinary actions taken against an IDEA student on the basis of a behavior contract.

[3]Dussault, William. "Functional Behavioral Assessment and Behavioral Intervention Plans." Fifteenth Annual Pacific Northwest Institute on Special Education and the Law (Yakima, WA. Sept. 28-30, 1998), p. 148-163.

Behavioral Intervention Plans (BIPs)

When a behavior intervention plan has been developed for a special education student, it becomes part of the student's IEP and the plan must be made known to all adults in the school environment who will need to implement it. Simply having a plan doesn't change behavior — implementing it does. Provisions should also be made for monitoring the implementation, as well as for crisis management, should that be necessary.

Many concerns about violating a student's privacy or confidentiality by sharing necessary information among school personnel are simply misplaced. A legal exception exists specifically to allow this sharing, with or without parental consent. IDEA properly requires that IEPs be accessible to all school employees who have a legitimate educational interest in them.

When a BIP has been developed for a student who has no IEP, it should be shared with all adults who need to know (see sidebar). Consistency in implementing every BIP is crucial to its success. In fact, inconsistency can actually cause the challenging behavior to become more severe and more frequent.

In order to develop a BIP, certain information is essential. The process of obtaining this data is the functional assessment of behavior. Depending on the complexity and intensity of the behavior of concern, more or less information may be helpful.

Initially, it is a good idea to ensure that all essential information is available and considered. On the following pages, we present an information gathering plan. It's followed by a Summary Statement. From the Summary Statement the BIP is developed. Six sample plans are presented in full — one each for a kindergarten, primary, elementary, upper grade, middle and high school student. They are presented in detail. A one-page flow chart recaps each plan. In the next chapter, a more streamlined approach is presented. As one becomes more experienced in recognizing the function of behaviors, the following information will be evident and doesn't necessarily have to be written.

Information to Develop an
Individual Student Support Plan

Student Name: _____ Grade: _____

Reported by: _____ Date: _____

1. Description of Student:

What are the strengths (e.g., academic, artistic, personal)? _____

What does he/she like to do (e.g., read books, play guitar, draw, do puzzles, ride skateboard, use computer)? _____

Who does he/she like (e.g., particular peer, principal, staff member)? _____

What food/drinks does he/she like? _____

What is home life like? _____

2. Present Level Functioning:

Which academic areas (e.g., reading, math, social studies) are working for him/her?

_____

Which academic areas are difficult for him/her? _____

How is he/she being helped in these areas? _____

What kind of social/behavioral problems does he/she have? _____

3. Describe the problems:

What does the behavior look like (e.g., hitting, cussing, running away)? _____

Where does he/she have problems (e.g., playground, cafeteria, classroom, locker area, before or after school)? _____

Who is usually around when the problem happens (e.g., teacher, assistant, peers)?

_____

What time of day does it usually happen? _____

4. What typically happens when he/she gets into trouble? _____

5. How often do these problems take place? _____

When as much as possible of the above information has been gathered, the following summary can be made:

Things that are going on at home or before the student gets to school that may have an effect later in the day (e.g., home stress, fight with parents/peers, lack of sleep, medication).

_____

What typically makes the student act inappropriately (e.g., a direction, a task, a person)?

_____

What does the student typically do that is inappropriate (e.g., talk back, whine, run away)?

_____

After the incident, what typically happens (e.g., send to office, time-out, parent contact, scolding)?

_____

Why does he/she misbehave (e.g. to get attention, to have power/control and/or to get out of doing a task)?

_____

Summary Statement

What might be happening at home or before school?	What sets him/her off?	What does he/she do that is not appropriate?	What happens right after the inappropriate behavior?	What does he/she want?
Setting Event	Predictor	Problem Behavior	Consequence	Maintaining Function

Six Stories (FBAs and BIPs):

Six plans follow which were developed by a real team for actual children. The teacher (and later district behavioral consultant), Dr. Golly, recalls the six stories.

1. Louis

Louis's mom moved into our district shortly before taking him out of his old school. After the IEP meeting and after hearing horror stories from Louis's teacher, I decided to go and visit him while still in his old school.

Louis was in a kindergarten classroom for children with language delays. The class had one teacher, two assistants and 12 students. Every day, Louis would become so non-compliant that the principal had to come and physically remove him from the classroom. He would be carried down the hall kicking and screaming.

When I observed, Louis was sitting cross-legged on the carpet. The teacher asked the children to introduce themselves to me. In the middle of the introductions, Louis raised his hand and told the teacher that he had been to the doctor. The teacher conversed with him for a few moments and continued the introduction task.

A few minutes later, the children had free play. Soon, Louis took away a toy from another student and hit him over the head. The assistant immediately came over and corrected Louis.

Louis's FBA Summary Statement

Setting Event	Predictor	Problem Behavior	Consequence	Maintaining Function
What might be happening at home or before school?	What sets him off?	What does he do that is not appropriate?	What happens right after the inappropriate behavior?	What does he want?
Lack of sleep.	Playing with other children.	Taking away toys, hitting, pushing, running around.	Teacher talks to him. When he starts running, the principal comes and physically removes him from the classroom.	Adult attention.

I concluded that Louis was getting a lot of attention for inappropriate behavior and decided to write the following behavior plan before he entered our school.

Behavior Plan For Louis

Louis will start in Mrs. B's regular kindergarten class on Tuesday, April 23rd. The Learning Center will provide Mrs. B with as much support as she needs the first 2 weeks.

Mrs. G, from the learning center, will teach Louis the following behaviors:

1. Raise hand without talking.

2. Do not interrupt others.

3. Share without aggression.

4. Follow teacher directions.

When Louis starts school on Tuesday, Mrs. G will explain the class rules to the assistant and to Louis. Louis will be shown examples and non-examples of the rules. During this session, Louis will be reinforced for listening and not talking out or interrupting. A Learning Center staff member will be in Room 3 to help facilitate his successful transition into Mrs. B's room. Penny and Darcey, who are assistants, will take turns working in Room 3 and will work cooperatively so that Mrs. B and her regular assistant can focus their attention on Louis and establish rapport with him. However, if Louis becomes non-compliant or aggressive, Penny or Darcey will take responsibility for following through with the consequences as outlined in the flowchart.

As soon as Louis is functioning successfully in the classroom, direct teacher support from the Learning Center will be gradually faded. If Mrs. B needs more than minimal support (assistant, high school student, parent volunteer), the Learning Center will provide the needed support until the end of the year.

We will have a short meeting on Fridays at 2:15 to discuss progress and concerns. Instructional assistants and staff members who work with Louis will keep a journal on their activities in Room 3. Penny, one of the assistants, will be available for the Friday meetings.

When Louis is with the rest of the class, the following flowchart procedures will be implemented as agreed to by the team (see flowchart on page 54).

Results:

Mrs. G role-played all the expectations with Louis. Only once was a "room clear" needed and the entire flowchart sequence implemented. From then on, Louis came into Room 14 to pet the rat (see flowchart) every day. He progressed well and did not need any extra behavior system the following year. Louis's family moved to another school district and Louis attended a different school for second grade. The last information we received was that he was progressing well.

Louis's flowchart

START 1 Did Louis follow class rules?

If Louis has more points on GREEN than on RED, and has not been sent to time-out for non-compliance, he earns being able to come to Room 14 before school is out to pet the rat. On Friday, he will get a small toy from the store in Room 14.

yes → Louis receives lots of praise & encouragement from all adults and points on green side of card.

no → Teacher restates expectation.

Did Louis comply?

yes → T says; "You made a good choice to come quietly." → Go to 1

no → Louis gets point on red side of card.

Did Louis comply?

yes → Reinforce Louis for making a good choice. → Go to 1

no → Say; "You need to go to Room 14."

Is Louis noncompliant & disruptive?

no → Louis stays in time-out for 5 min. → Go to 1

yes → Mrs. B asks rest of class to line up for extra recess (room clear).

Did Louis calm down within 10 min. & go to time-out?

yes → Mrs. B returns with class. Louis stays in time-out for 10 min. → Go to 1

no → Adult calls Room 14 to assist in physical removal of Louis. → Louis has lost privilege to be in Room 3 for rest of day & stays in a quiet place.

2. Anlee

Anlee, an extremely bright first grader, had been through the First Step to Success (Walker, Stiller, Golly, Kavanaugh, Severson, & Feil, 1997) program in kindergarten while she was at a previous school. One of the components of the First Step to Success program teaches students appropriate behaviors through role-play and feedback. Anlee had been successful with that program but needed a "booster shot." She displayed problem behaviors such as arguing, whining, tantrumming and screaming on a daily basis. She had made friends with Jeanne, a 4th grader at the present school.

The team decided that Anlee needed to work on the following replacement behaviors:

1. Raise hand quietly to get teacher attention.

2. Keep control of self (no crying/ screaming).

3. Follow teacher directions within 10 seconds the first time asked.

4. Cooperate with other students.

Anlee's FBA Summary Statement

Setting Event	Predictor	Problem Behavior	Consequence	Maintaining Function
What might be happening at home or before school?	What sets her off?	What does she do that is not appropriate?	What happens right after the inappropriate behavior?	What does she want?
Single working mom, only child.	Teacher request.	She argues and/or has a temper tantrum.	Teacher keeps argument going and when a tantrum follows, Anlee is removed from class to time-out.	Adult attention.

Behavior Plan For Anlee

Jeanne and Anlee will design a point chart. Anlee will carry the chart and ask her teachers to mark points earned for each period. For every point earned, Anlee gets 1 minute special time with Jeanne.

Anlee will follow the same expectations and general classroom management plan as other students. Mrs. G will teach the expectations and consequences on Monday at 9:50.

If Anlee has a tantrum, argues or pouts, the teacher will do a room clear and take all students except Anlee to the playground or library. An assistant from Room 14 will come over to supervise Anlee but will not talk to her unless she is calm and sitting quietly in her seat looking at a book. Anlee will make up wasted time during a "fun" activity. She will go to Room 14 (there is an adult in Room14 at all times.) during Friday Fun Club or during another "preferred" activity. The idea is to have her in a "boring" environment when she is making up wasted time.

Teachers will pre-correct Anlee and "set her up" for a successful day each morning. The following will be implemented starting Monday:

Anlee will come to Room 14 at 8:10. Mrs. G will role-play classroom rules as follows:

Rule 1: Listen to the teacher.

Expectation: When the teacher says, "*May I have your attention please?*", put hands on desk or in lap and eyes on teacher without talking.

Negative examples:

- Continue cutting with scissors.
- Hands in desk instead of on desk.
- Talking while waiting.
- Waiting too long to stop working.

Rule 2: Raise your hand

Expectation: When you need to say something or ask for help, raise your hand without talking and stay seated to get teacher help.

Negative examples:

- Shouting out while raising hand (saying, *"I need a drink!"*).
- Getting out of seat.

Additional classroom expectations:

- Students sharpen pencils in the morning. They can't sharpen pencils during the day. There are always sharp pencils in the room to be used.

- It's OK to ask for a drink during seat work but NEVER when the teacher is giving directions or talking.

- When the teacher explains things, students must listen and can't raise hands.

Rule 3: Keep hands and feet to self.

Expectation: Touch only your own belongings unless you have permission from the teacher or other students to touch their things. When you want to talk to others, ask for their attention rather than pulling on their clothes or hitting them. When someone else touches you, ask him politely to stop. For example, *"Please don't touch my head."*

Negative examples:

- Getting upset when things touch you.
- Wailing

Note: When sent back to seat for inappropriate behavior, don't make comments and say, *"Don't laugh at me!"* Just go to your seat without talking.

Anlee wants control, so we need to provide this by giving her opportunities such as choosing a partner to go out to recess with her and Jeanne. Later, we need to teach her to work cooperatively in a group.

On Monday at 9:50, the classroom teacher will review classroom expectations. Anlee and Mrs. G will be there as well so everyone knows the expectations. This will minimize her opportunities to argue about what is expected.

The teacher will provide Mrs. G with feedback at the end of the week and discuss changes if necessary.

Results:

Anlee carried her point card for one week and received all possible points. The team (including Anlee and Jeanne) decided that Anlee would have regular recess breaks with Jeanne unless she had an infraction (e.g., talk-back, tantrum), and they would discontinue the card. Anlee had two major temper tantrums during the remainder of the year, once in the cafeteria and once in her reading class.

Anlee is currently a model student in seventh grade. She is in the talented and gifted (TAG) program, has lots of friends and loves school.

Anlee's Point Chart

	Mon.	Tues.	Wed.	Thurs.	Fri.	Comments
Opening	2					
Reading	1					
Language Arts	2					
Social Studies	1					
Lunch Time	2					
P.E./Music	2					
Math	2					
Science	1					
Clean-up	2					
Total Points	15					
Time earned with Jeanne	15 minutes					
Comments	Anlee spent 15 minutes after school helping Jeanne plant flowers in 5th grade garden area.					

START

Anlee's flowchart

1 — Is Anlee following directions?

yes → Provide Anlee with positive feedback.

no → Give Anlee a clear direction, e.g., "Read the story on pg. 5 quietly to yourself."

Provide Anlee with positive feedback. ↓ Is the class period over?

Is the class period over? — no → Go to 1

Is the class period over? — yes → Put points on card.

Put points on card. ↓ Is the school day finished?

Is the school day finished? — no → Go to 1

Is the school day finished? — yes → Add up points & finish chart.

Add up points & finish chart. ↓ Did Anlee earn time with Jeanne?

Did Anlee earn time with Jeanne? — no → Go to 1

Did Anlee earn time with Jeanne? — yes → Decide when she can spend time with Jeanne.

Decide when she can spend time with Jeanne. → Go to 1

Did Anlee follow directions? — yes → Go to 1

Did Anlee follow directions? — no → Is Anlee being disrespectful? (tantrums, shouts, pouts).

Is Anlee being disrespectful? (tantrums, shouts, pouts). — no → Go to 1

Is Anlee being disrespectful? (tantrums, shouts, pouts). — yes → Notice time and ignore behavior. 2

Notice time and ignore behavior. 2 → Can behavior be ignored?

Can behavior be ignored? — yes → Go to 2

Can behavior be ignored? — no → Take rest of class out of room to playground & ask adult to supervise Anlee.

Take rest of class out of room to playground & ask adult to supervise Anlee. ↓ Is Anlee calm & following directions? 3

Is Anlee calm & following directions? 3 — yes → Mark on card how many minutes she owes.

Mark on card how many minutes she owes. ↓ Anlee makes up time in Room 14 during preferred activity.

Is Anlee calm & following directions? 3 — no → Continue to keep track of time owed. Minimize attention.

Continue to keep track of time owed. Minimize attention. → Go to 3

3. Jose

Jose was an active and bright second grader who loved computers. He was identified as a student with Attention Deficit Disorder with Hyperactivity (ADHD) before he entered kindergarten. Jose received medication for his condition.

Even with his medication, Jose still needed to learn many social behaviors when he entered kindergarten. He and his parents participated in the First Step to Success program and did well. Jose continued to do well in first grade and until the middle of the year in second grade when he started to have daily problems on the bus.

Jose's FBA Summary Statement

Setting Event	Predictor	Problem Behavior	Consequence	Maintaining Function
What might be happening at home or before school?	What sets him off?	What does he do that is not appropriate?	What happens right after the inappropriate behavior?	What does he want?
Mom easy going, stepdad strict. One baby sister. Taking Ritalin for hyperactivity.	Sitting on the bus.	Inappropriate language, obscene gestures.	Bus driver stops bus and scolds Jose. Other students laugh. After bus ride, the bus driver tells teacher or parents about problems.	Peer and adult attention.

The team, including the bus driver, designed the following plan:

Behavior Plan For Jose

1. Teach Jose the expected bus behavior. The bus driver will help with this, and we will model for Jose on the actual bus that he rides.

2. Jose will be seated in the first seat on the right of the bus driver.

3. The bus driver will have a large card which is RED on one side and GREEN on the other.

4. When Jose follows directions on the bus, the driver will occasionally hold up the GREEN card and when Jose has done a good job, the bus driver will give him a small green ticket.

5. If Jose does not follow directions, the bus driver will hold up the RED card. If Jose changes his behavior, the card will go back to GREEN. If he doesn't change his behavior, the bus driver will give him a small red ticket at the end of the bus ride.

6. Jose will hand the tickets to Mrs. G. He can earn 5 minutes of computer time for each green ticket. He can save up his green tickets and negotiate computer time with his teacher.

7. When Jose has 3 red tickets, another meeting will be scheduled to discuss an alternative plan.

8. Jose will be allowed to read books or play with a small toy during the bus ride.

Results:

The plan worked for about 4 months. The last month of school, Jose got in a fight with a child at his bus stop. When Jose entered the bus after the fight, he would not follow the driver's directions. He received 3 tickets in a row and lost his privilege to ride the regular education bus. He was moved to a special education bus for a week.

After that week, we continued the GREEN/RED card program. Jose did well for the remainder of the year.

Jose's flowchart

START

```
Show the                 yes      ┌─────────────┐      no      Show the RED card.
GREEN card.        ◄─────────────│      1      │─────────────►
                                  │     Is      │
                                  │ Jose following │
                                  │  bus rules? │
      │                           └─────────────┘                        │
      ▼                                                                   ▼
Give Jose a GREEN                                                    ┌─────────────┐
ticket at end of ride.           Give Jose RED ticket      no        │     Did     │
                                  at end of ride.    ◄──────────────│ Jose do the right │
      │                                                              │    thing?   │
      ▼                                  │                           └─────────────┘
Jose gives tickets to                    │                                 │ yes
Ms. G. Each ticket                       │                                 ▼
is 5 min. of                             │                          Turn card to GREEN.  ──►  Go to 1
computer time.                           │
      │                                  ▼
      ▼                           ┌─────────────┐      yes
Teacher sends Jose to             │    Has      │─────────────► Call meeting for new plan.
Room 14 for                       │ Jose received 3 │
computer time.                    │ RED tickets? │
                                  └─────────────┘
                                         │ no
                                         ▼
                                  Continue plan.
```

63

4. Michael

Michael was a good-looking fifth grader who played football and was well-liked by his peers. He gained control of the classroom and got attention from his peers by being silly behind the teacher's back. It was difficult for the teacher to gain class control when Michael was in one of his "silly" modes.

Michael's FBA Summary Statement

Setting Event	Predictor	Problem Behavior	Consequence	Maintaining Function
What might be happening at home or before school?	What sets him off?	What does he do that is not appropriate?	What happens right after the inappropriate behavior?	What does he want?
Dad in jail, mom dysfunctional.	When teacher is not looking.	Michael acts silly, makes obscene gestures and inappropriate noises.	When asked to stop, he ignores the teacher. He continues to be silly. Peers laugh at him and want him to continue.	Peer/adult attention.

The team came up with the following plan:

Behavior Plan For Michael

Michael has decided that he wants to act more maturely in school and get attention for appropriate behavior. Michael's teacher and Mrs. G have agreed to help Michael make better choices. The following plan will be implemented:

Michael will follow directions in a mature way (no line-dancing, noises, faces). Michael will stay on task during class time and work quietly at his desk. When Michael needs teacher attention, he will raise his hand quietly. Michael will show respect to his teachers and others.

Every morning, Michael will come to Mrs. G's room to get a daily point chart and will be at spelling on time (7:50). Michael will be responsible for asking teachers for feedback on his card after each period. He can earn a + or – for each period. It's Michael's responsibility to keep track of his card.

If Michael earns a + for every period before lunch, he earns a "Super" ticket. If he earns a + for every period after lunch, he earns another "super" ticket. The next morning, he will show his card to Mrs. G and she will post the "Super" tickets in Room 14. As soon as Michael has earned 10 "Super" tickets, he can have lunch with a school staff member of his choice.

Michael's teacher will give him attention when Michael is following directions, working quietly at his seat and making good choices when interacting with other students.

After Michael has earned his first lunch date, we will meet and set a new goal for him. Michael and his teacher will sign this plan indicating their agreement to follow it.

Michael's Chart

	Mon.	Tues.	Wed.	Thurs.	Fri.	Comments
Period:	Date:					
7:50 – 8:20						
8:20 – 9:10						
9:10 – 10:10						
Recess						
10:30 – 11:15						
11:15 – 12:00						
Lunch/Recess	Super morning yes/no	Super morning yes/no	Super morning yes/no	Super morning yes/no	Super morning yes/no	
12:30 – 1:15						
1:15 – 2:00						
	Super yes/no	Super yes/no	Super yes/no	Super yes/no	Super yes/no	

Results:

Michael earned two lunch dates. After the second, he decided he didn't need to carry the card anymore. We told him that we would continue to keep track of his behavior and meet when necessary.

See next page for Michael's flowchart:

START

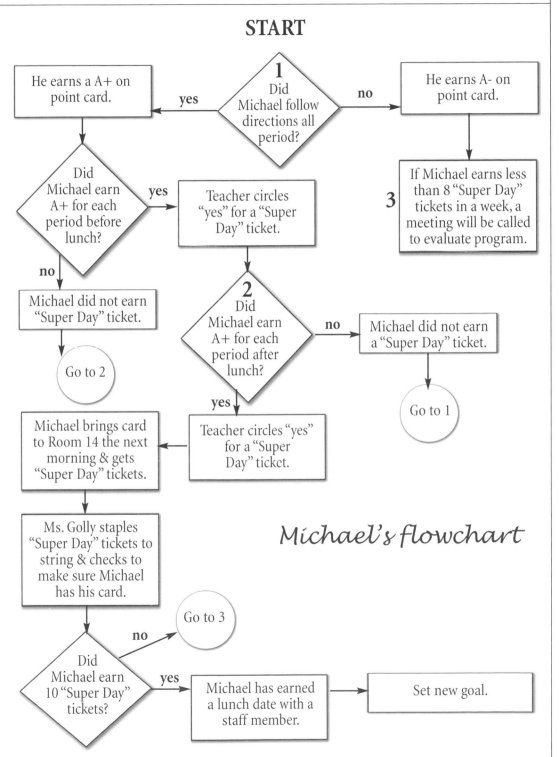

1 Did Michael follow directions all period?

He earns a A+ on point card.

He earns A- on point card.

Did Michael earn A+ for each period before lunch?

Teacher circles "yes" for a "Super Day" ticket.

3 If Michael earns less than 8 "Super Day" tickets in a week, a meeting will be called to evaluate program.

Michael did not earn "Super Day" ticket.

Go to 2

2 Did Michael earn A+ for each period after lunch?

Michael did not earn a "Super Day" ticket.

Go to 1

Michael brings card to Room 14 the next morning & gets "Super Day" tickets.

Teacher circles "yes" for a "Super Day" tickct.

Ms. Golly staples "Super Day" tickets to string & checks to make sure Michael has his card.

Michael's flowchart

Go to 3

Did Michael earn 10 "Super Day" tickets?

Michael has earned a lunch date with a staff member.

Set new goal.

5. Tess

Tess, a bright fifth grader, had been living with her biological father in another state, where she attended a private school for girls.

Tess came to live with her mom and stepdad and attended the neighborhood school. Tess loved her mom but hated living with her mom and stepdad. She tried to get in trouble so she would be sent back to her real dad (according to Tess). Her behaviors escalated to violent acts (throwing objects, hurting others, bringing a knife to school). Tess was expelled from her neighborhood school and enrolled in our school.

Mom informed us before Tess enrolled in school in November that we should anticipate non-compliant and aggressive behaviors. According to mom, there was no possibility for Tess to return to her dad in the near future.

Tess's FBA Summary Statement

Setting Event	Predictor	Problem Behavior	Consequence	Maintaining Function
What might be happening at home or before school?	What sets her off?	What does she do that is not appropriate?	What happens right after the inappropriate behavior?	What does she want?
Tess has arguments with stepdad every morning. She wants to go and live with her biological dad in another state.	Teacher request and independent work.	She refuses to do her work. She argues, is defiant and has severe talk outs using foul language, hurtful comments, and she sometimes destroys property (e.g., tears pages out of books, scratches graffiti on desk).	Teacher asks her to go to time-out.	She wants to avoid going to this particular school. She wants to be sent back to California.

With mom's input, we designed the following plan and contract for Tess:

Behavior Plan For Tess

Tess will start school on Monday, in Room 9. Her home room teacher will be Mrs. B. All 4th and 5th graders (approximately 150 students) are in the QUEST unit. Tess may earn QUEST privileges (field trips, special events & activities). She also may be grouped in one of the other four QUEST teachers' classes for specific activities.

Tess's daily schedule will be as follows:

  7:50 – Have backpack checked in Room 14.

       – Line-up in front of Room 9.

       – Enter room quietly when invited.

During this time Tess has permission to sharpen pencils, go to the bathroom and get a drink. She may not bother others or use computers.

  8:00 – Be in seat.

       – Do "warm-up" activity from overhead.

       – Listen for teacher directions.

  8:30 – Math

  9:30 – Recess

  9:45 – Music (M&W), PE (T & Th), Class meeting (F)

10:15 – Home room (rotation after Winter Break)

11:00 –Home room

11:45 – Lunch and Recess

12:25 – Writing and Reading

  1:55 – Have backpack checked before dismissal.

  2:05 – Homework Club (& snack)

Behavior Agreement For Tess

I, Tess, want to be successful at school. If I follow school and classroom rules, I can earn points. I can earn 5 points for each period (see point chart). I can earn 55 points every day. I must earn at least 45 points every day for a special privilege.

Mrs. B will write down points when she sees me doing the right thing (see rules). She will give me opportunities throughout the day to see how many points I have earned.

I can also earn points during each recess, lunch and other QUEST classes. The teachers on duty will keep Mrs. B informed of my behaviors in places other than Room 9.

If I choose not to follow the rules, I will follow the consequences outlined on the enclosed flowcharts (see flowcharts 1 and 2).

I understand this contract and agree with the conditions:

Tess: _____   Teacher: _____

I would like to earn one of the following privileges if I have earned at least 45 points:

I am also interested in earning the following privileges if I make mature choices for 3 days in a row. And I never know when I'll get a surprise if I follow directions!

Results:

Tess came to school with her mom for a formal meeting the evening before the first day at her new school. The meeting was video-taped and attended by the principal, QUEST teachers and the resource teacher. The team wanted to let Tess know that the goal was to help her be successful, teach her what she needed to know to be successful and give her a new start.

After the meeting, the teacher showed her the classroom and explained expectations. Tess immediately "fell in love" with the animals (pet rats, guinea pigs and frogs) in the room.

The classroom teacher had prepared the rest of the class before Tess's arrival and had asked students to be kind and supportive. The class was extremely supportive and Tess became popular. She gained one inseparable friend and the two of them became class leaders. Tess's behavior was nearly exemplary for the rest of the school year.

Taking care of the rats was reinforcing. In fact, Tess earned points to go to the pet store with her teacher to buy another class rat after three perfect days. She loved taking care of the rats, and that was the only reward she requested during the next month. After that, she did not need a point card. She continued to take care of the pets.

Tess continued to have difficulties at home with her stepdad. After completing 5th grade successfully, she went back to live with her biological dad. She returned for a visit when she was in 7th grade. She looked great and was doing well in school.

Tess's Chart

	Line up	Opening	Math	Recess	Music PE	Rm9	Rm9	Lunch	Read	Bonus	Total
	7:45-8:00	8:00-8:25	8:30-9:30	9:30-9:45	9:45-10:15	10:15-11:00	11:00-11:45	11:45-12:25	12:25-1:55		
Points	5	5	5	5	5	5	5	5	5		
Mon.											
Tues.											
Wed.											
Thurs.											
Fri.											

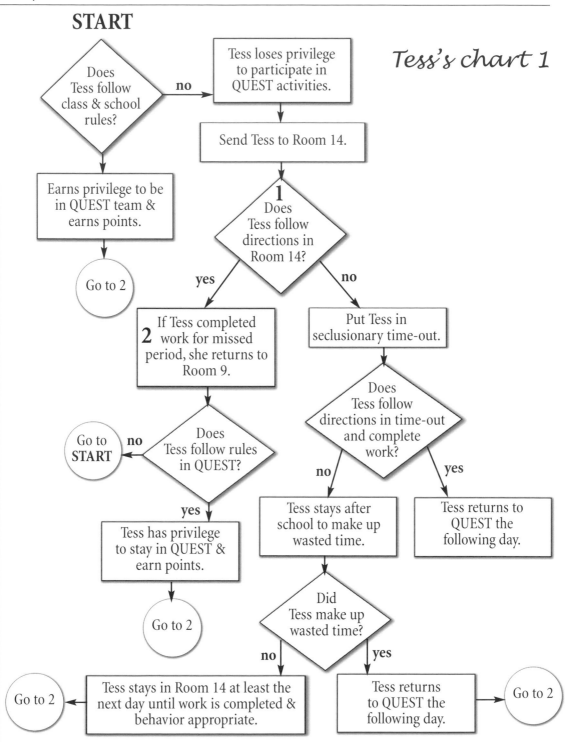

START

Tess's chart 1

Does Tess follow class & school rules?

no → Tess loses privilege to participate in QUEST activities.

Send Tess to Room 14.

Earns privilege to be in QUEST team & earns points.

Go to 2

1 Does Tess follow directions in Room 14?

yes → **2** If Tess completed work for missed period, she returns to Room 9.

no → Put Tess in seclusionary time-out.

Does Tess follow directions in time-out and complete work?

no → Tess stays after school to make up wasted time.

yes → Tess returns to QUEST the following day.

Does Tess follow rules in QUEST?

Go to START ← no

yes → Tess has privilege to stay in QUEST & earn points.

Go to 2

Did Tess make up wasted time?

no → Tess stays in Room 14 at least the next day until work is completed & behavior appropriate.

Go to 2 ←

yes → Tess returns to QUEST the following day.

→ Go to 2

Tess's chart 2

START

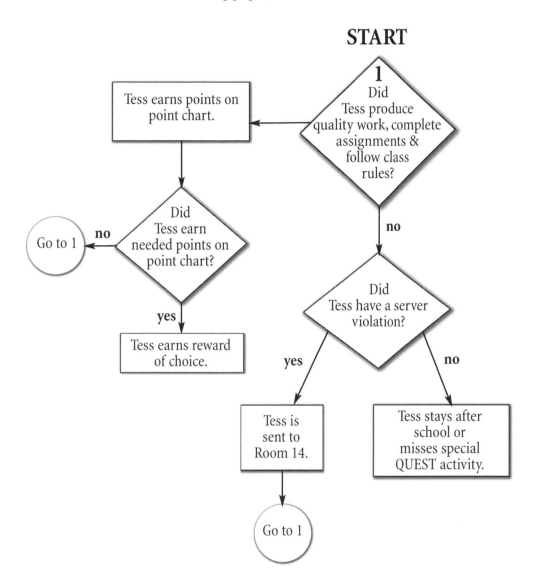

1
Did Tess produce quality work, complete assignments & follow class rules?

Tess earns points on point chart.

no

Did Tess earn needed points on point chart?

no → Go to 1

Did Tess have a server violation?

yes → Tess earns reward of choice.

yes → Tess is sent to Room 14.

no → Tess stays after school or misses special QUEST activity.

Go to 1

6. Len

Len was a 17 year old high school student. He was an average student, but not popular. Other students reported his inappropriate behavior on a daily basis. He often bragged about material possessions and about his unethical computer hacking. He was overweight and not very athletic. He enjoyed chess although he was not very good at it.

The counselor spoke with the school chess club and asked if anyone was willing to volunteer, as an earned privilege, to teach chess to a student who was having problems. Whoever volunteered could earn "community service" credits. Two students said they were interested.

Len's FBA Summary Statement

Setting Event	Predictor	Problem Behavior	Consequence	Maintaining Function
What might be happening at home or before school?	What sets him off?	What does he do that is not appropriate?	What happens right after the inappropriate behavior?	What does he want?
Upper middle class family. Two working professional parents & three younger siblings.	Other students around.	Inappropriate language (e.g., cussing, put downs).	Peers push him away and cuss back. If teacher is around, Len is sent to the office.	Peer attention.

The team developed the following plan for Len:

Behavior Plan For Len

The counselor would role-play appropriate and inappropriate ways for Len to get peer attention. During the role-play, the counselor would act as Len, and Len would act as another student. When Len was comfortable with the role-play, two students from the drama club would join and act as peers. The role plays would include examples of appropriate and inappropriate ways of getting peer attention, including the use of cuss words and put-downs. Specific examples would be used to show Len clearly what was and was not acceptable.

The counselor would check with Len's teachers each day for reports of inappropriate language use. For each good report day, Len could earn 15 minutes of chess time with a chess club peer. Len could save the earned 15 minute privileges for up to 2 hours of chess sessions. He could negotiate with the peer the maximum amount of time allowed at each session. The supervising teacher of the chess club told Len the behaviors that were expected in chess club.

The first week, Len earned 45 minutes. Before the chess game, the peer was instructed to treat Len with respect. If Len used inappropriate language, the peer was asked not to give eye contact, but casually say, "We don't use that kind of language here" and to continue playing and quickly say something positive about the game.

Results:

Len felt special being invited into the chess club. His behavior was very appropriate and improved quickly. He used the computer for chess games and also to gain information. After three weeks, Len's inappropriate language was not reported any more. He eventually joined the chess club as a member in good standing.

Len's chart

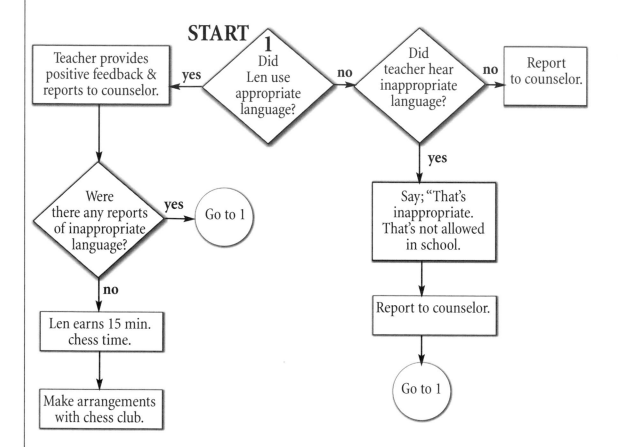

START

1 Did Len use appropriate language?

— **yes** → Teacher provides positive feedback & reports to counselor.

— **no** → Did teacher hear inappropriate language?

Did teacher hear inappropriate language? — **no** → Report to counselor.

Did teacher hear inappropriate language? — **yes** → Say; "That's inappropriate. That's not allowed in school.

Teacher provides positive feedback & reports to counselor. → Were there any reports of inappropriate language?

Were there any reports of inappropriate language? — **yes** → Go to 1

Were there any reports of inappropriate language? — **no** → Len earns 15 min. chess time.

Len earns 15 min. chess time. → Make arrangements with chess club.

Say; "That's inappropriate. That's not allowed in school. → Report to counselor.

Report to counselor. → Go to 1

Chapter IV

Measuring Behavioral Progress

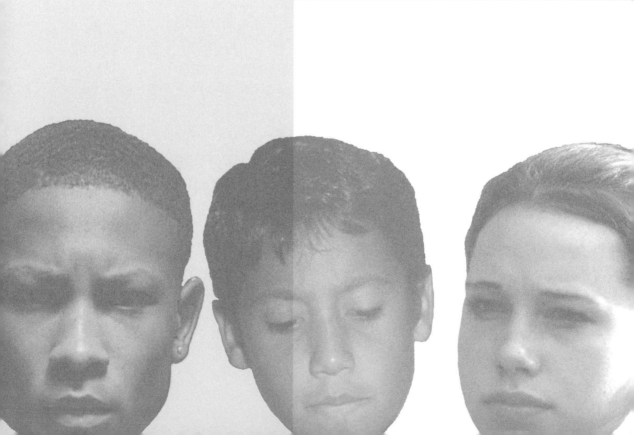

Measuring Behavioral Progress[4]

If your child isn't feeling well and her forehead seems hot to your touch, what do you do? You probably **measure**, i.e., take her temperature. Suppose it's 102°. You do all the right things, and later her face feels cooler to your hand. To be sure, you take her temperature again. It's 98.6°. Good news, and you are assured the change is in the right direction.

You've joined a weight watching program. You know the rest . . . measure, measure, measure. An acquaintance of yours bought some stock and now checks each day to see how well it's doing. Be it degrees, pounds, or dollars, all are ways of counting/measuring.

> *Once a behavioral intervention plan (BIP) has been developed and implemented, we need to know how successful it is. This requires measuring the results.*

B.J. sulks, pouts, and mumbles to himself so much his teacher is concerned. The teacher develops a plan to reduce this behavior and reports a month later he now does those things 10 – 20 minutes a day. Is that progress? Is the teacher's plan effective? Clearly, we don't know until we know how many minutes a day he sulked and pouted **before** the plan.

When the concern is Kenny's use of vulgar language in the classroom, we need to know if he does it once a semester or several times daily. Without knowing that, we can't judge progress in his usage.

Once a behavioral intervention plan (BIP) has been developed and implemented, we need to know how successful it is. This requires measuring the results. Whether the BIP has been developed for a regular or special education student, it's important to know if and when it has been successful if it needs to be modified. Additionally, IDEA requires that when a special education student has behavioral-social-emotional needs, they must be addressed on the student's IEP, i.e., measurable goals and objectives must be included. Furthermore, progress must be reported to parents,

---

[4]Some of the material in this chapter is adapted from portions of Bateman, B., & Herr, C. (2003). *Writing Measurable IEP Goals and Objectives.* Verona, WI: Attainment.

including whether that progress is sufficient to achieve the goal by the end of the year. The BIP is the instructional plan designed to move the student from the present level of performance of specific behaviors to the goal level.

If a BIP is effective, the student's challenging behaviors will become less frequent and severe and the appropriate replacement behaviors will become more frequent. To know if this is happening, someone must measure the results of implementing the BIP.

To measure the effectiveness of any behavior intervention, it must be known how long or how frequently it occurs before and after the intervention. However, "how long" and "how frequently" can be assessed on a variety of scales. Using only a subjective approach, the teacher might report, "I feel that Carlos is doing better this week. His attitude seems somewhat improved." A teacher using objective measurement could report, "Last week Carlos earned three stickers for appropriate language during recess. This week he earned eight." An even more meaningful measure would be that before the BIP Carlos averaged 12 inappropriate words during recess, and after two weeks, he averaged less than one. However, we need to be aware that some people prefer to specify, record, or count only the appropriate replacement behavior, not the inappropriate target behavior. This is consistent with the larger principle of paying attention to the desired behaviors. There may be times, however, when the efficiency of tracking the inappropriate behavior outweighs other considerations. Our view is that measuring, counting, and recording are so important that, however they are done, consistent with common sense and respect, is better than not doing them. Certainly, whenever it is reasonable, the major focus should be on the positive behaviors.

> *Measuring, counting, and recording are so important that, however they are done — consistent with common sense and respect — it's better than not doing them.*

Measurable behaviors are observable and countable. We often think first in non-measurable terms. We use words like attitude, motivation or respect. We know the behaviors that contribute to a student showing a poor attitude, being poorly motivated, or lacking respect for authority. It is just exactly those behaviors that need to be specified. What behaviors make us believe Michael has a "poor attitude?"

Perhaps he often doesn't answer when spoken to, makes contemptuous facial expressions, slouches in his desk with arms crossed and eyes closed, and responds slowly or not at all. Those are the behaviors of concern.

> *Another key consideration is whether, if several people evaluated the student's performance, they would all come to the same conclusion about accomplishment of the BG/O.*

"Measurable" is an essential characteristic of a behavioral goal or objective (BG/O). If a BG/O isn't measurable, it can't be measured. If it can't be measured, we can't be sure when progress has been made.

To measure something is to perform a particular operation, to **do** something. To measure one's weight, one stands on a scale. To measure temperature, one looks at a thermometer. To measure tire pressure, one puts a gauge on the valve stem. And on and on. To measure is to perform an action of some type. An important question to always keep in mind, in writing measurable BG/Os, is, "What would one **do** to see if the child has accomplished this BG/O?"

Another key consideration is whether, if several people evaluated the student's performance, they would all come to the same conclusion about accomplishment of the BG/O.

> *When the BG/O is measured, we must be able to say how much progress has been made since the intervention began.*

If the goal were that Rocky would learn "to cope appropriately with being teased," evaluators could easily disagree over whether certain responses to teasings demonstrated appropriate coping. However, if the goal were that "when teased, Rocky would make no verbal response and would walk away," observers would be more likely to agree.

A third critical issue is that when the BG/O is measured, we must be able to say how much progress has been made since the intervention began or a previous BG/O was measured. "How much" requires some degree or level of quantification. This is not to say we must insert 80% (or any other %) into every BG/O! Doing that routinely, as many people do, has some sad and some absurd results, as we'll see shortly.

One further characteristic of a measurable BG/O is that it can be measured as it is written, without having to refer to additional, external information. Whether a student can "count to 10 without error" can be determined as readily as it is stated. But "will improve counting skill" cannot be assessed without additional information about the previous counting skill level. It also fails to indicate how much improvement, i.e., to what level, will satisfy the goal.

In sum, a measurable BG/O:

    1. Reveals what to do to **measure** whether the BG/O has been accomplished;

    2. Yields the same conclusion if measured by **several** people;

    3. Allows a calculation of **how much** progress it represents; and

    4. Can be measured **without** additional information.

These four characteristics describe measurability. In addition to fitting these criteria, a measurable BG/O contains (1) an observable learner performance (what the learner will be doing, such as counting, writing, pointing, describing), (2) measurable criteria which specify the **level** at which student performance will be acceptable (speed, accuracy, frequency, quality), and (3) important conditions of the performance such as "given software," or "given access to a dictionary."

If a BG/O needs a given or a condition, it's usually stated first. The learner's performance is often stated next, and the desired level of performance or criteria is stated last, for example:

    Given a 15 minute recess period (given),

    Jason will appropriately initiate interaction (performance) with at least one peer (criterion)

A frequently problematic element of BG/Os for many of us is the **observable, visible or countable behavior** requirement. Here are some examples of observable and not observable behaviors:

Observable	*Not observable*
matching author to book title	*appreciating* art
reading orally	*enjoying* literature
constructing a timeline	*understanding* history
dressing one's self	*becoming* independent
speaking to adults without vulgarities	*respecting* authority
pointing, drawing, identifying, writing, etc.	*improving, feeling, knowing*

Of course, we hope our students will appreciate, enjoy, understand, respect and more. Of that there is no doubt. But for purposes of goals and objectives, we must ask ourselves what we hope to **see** — the behavior visible to us and others — that we'll accept as indicating that our student is appreciating nature, enjoying literature, or being respectful to adults.

> *The most abused criterion, beyond a doubt, is percentage. For example, Benny will "use three anger management skills with 80% accuracy."*
>
> *What good will it do Benny to use three anger management skills only partially correctly, and what is accuracy in anger management?*

The criterion is simply how well the learner must do, the level of performance required to meet the goal. It is the height to which the performance must rise, or the depth to which it must fall (if digging a 3' deep post hole) to be successful. Frequently used criteria include 4 of 5 trials, 3 consecutive days, once a day, etc. The most abused criterion, beyond a doubt, is percentage. For example, Benny will "use three anger management skills with 80% accuracy," or Kenny will "maintain appropriate eye contact with 90% accuracy." What good will it do Benny to use three anger management skills only partially correctly, and what is accuracy in anger management? How will you measure whether Kenny maintains eye contact with 90% accuracy and what is accuracy in eye contact? The history of how this strange usage began appears to be lost, but we now have to bury the custom. Never again should Don be expected to "improve his behavior with 75% accuracy," nor Annabel required to "improve her behavior 80% of the time."

Just as measurability is essential, so non-measurability must be diligently avoided. Some actual real-world examples of non-measurable goals make this point.

Rebecca will become more cooperative in the classroom.

This BG/O has no criterion to indicate the level at which Rebecca must perform to reach the goal, nor does it specify the behavior of being "cooperative." If two or more people tried to determine if Rebecca had accomplished this, they might well disagree with each other. Even if we knew what this goal writer meant by "more cooperative," we could not tell if Rebecca had "improved" without knowing the previous level of her cooperation. Thousands and thousands of goals use this "student will improve in X" format. It is not measurable, not acceptable and not useful. To improve this BG/O, we ask what the writer probably meant. What might Rebecca do that would make us think she is "cooperating"? Perhaps "immediately doing what the teacher asks" would be an acceptable, visible learner performance. Possibly this measurable version is close to what was intended: Given 5 simple directions such as "Please hand in your paper," Rebecca will correctly complete 4 of the 5 directions, without hesitation or inappropriate verbalization.

Kevin will decrease his inappropriate remarks to other children 90% of the time.

"Decrease his inappropriate remarks" is indeed a visible learner performance, but what in the world is "90% of the time"?? This is utter gibberish. Suppose Kevin makes an average of 10 inappropriate remarks daily. Presumably this gibberish writer intended to reduce that by 90 percent, i.e., to have Kevin make no more than one inappropriate remark daily. If so, that is exactly what should have been said: Kevin will make no more than one inappropriate remark to other children daily.

Granted, "inappropriate" is a wee bit vague and could lead to an occasional difference of opinion among evaluators. Nevertheless, it is well within the boundaries we're comfortable with in our real world.

Max will be 75% successful in the classroom.

In this BG/O we see the common and utterly false belief that including a percentage (typically between 70 and 90) somehow makes a BG/O measurable. Nothing could be further from the truth. Think about exactly **how** you would **measure** it. What would you **count** to know if Max had been successful in a given class or week? If it can't be **objectively assessed**, it isn't measurable! What did the writer mean? Perhaps that Max would pass three of his four classes. If so, that is what should be said: Max will pass three of the four regular education classes he takes. Or, perhaps the writer meant Max would be sent to the office for disciplinary reasons no more than one day in four. If so, that is what should have been said.

Sara will make wise choices in her use of leisure time.

Sara may, indeed "make wise choices," but we really can't see her doing this. There is no visible learner performance here, nor is there a criterion. Perhaps the writer meant something like: Sara will attend a supervised, school-sponsored extra-curricular activity at least once a week.

Anthony will work within a group setting without demonstrating overt behaviors directed at others unless these behaviors are mandated by the group session.

Surely we don't think this way, do we? Perhaps the truth is that the writer was browsing software objectives, hoping to find something that might fit Anthony. How much better to start with Anthony, as we know him. He bothers other children verbally and physically when they're working. How often does he do this? At least 20-25 times a day. Does this suggest a goal? It should. How about "Anthony will not bother other children inappropriately, verbally or physically, when they are working?" Why 'inappropriately?' Because he might need information or assistance and ask for it very appropriately — a behavior we don't want to discourage. And when we say he will not do it, that is the criterion — zero "bothers."

J.B. will use at least two strategies to take responsibility for his anger management with 80% accuracy.

What in the world did this writer really have in mind? Possibly something like "J.B. will have no inappropriate displays of anger." Why not say it just like that? The writer might object saying, "I don't expect J.B. to be perfect." OK. How **often** should J.B. have an inappropriate display of anger by the end of a full year of reteaching? Perhaps no more than 1 a month, since he now has 2 or 3 every day.

A brief word is necessary about reporting to parents the measured progress a special education student makes toward a behavioral goal. Progress of students on IEPs must be reported to their parents as often as that of other students is reported. Usually this is every six or nine weeks. These reports must address whether the progress made is sufficient for the student to accomplish the goal by the end of the year. A simple way to satisfy this requirement is to use a "ladder" with the present performance as the bottom rung, the grading period objectives as the middle rungs, and the goal as the top rung, as seen in Fig. 2. Each grading period, the actual performance is assessed and entered on the appropriate rung of the ladder and a copy sent to the parents.

Fig. 2 Behavior Ladder

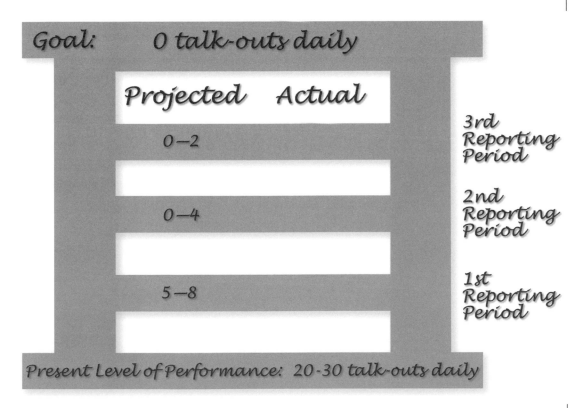

A copy of this ladder meets both good practice and legal requirements. Notice that the top rung is labeled goal rather than annual goal. Many inappropriate behaviors will be replaced by appropriate ones in less than one year. When a behavior plan has been developed, its effectiveness can usually be determined within a week or so and changes made if necessary. Most behavioral goals, therefore, have maintenance as the annual goal, with a shorter term for initially reaching criterion.

In the following chapter, many examples of streamlined behavior intervention plans are presented, each with a brief comment and discussion of the measurement considerations it presents.

Chapter V

Basic Plans

Basic Plans

Once a teacher or an IEP team is thoroughly comfortable with the behavior management practices and principles discussed so far, a basic or streamlined behavioral intervention plan may be appropriate in many situations. Of course, if such a plan is not successful, it will need to be revised. Under some circumstances IDEA may require that a functional behavioral analysis be conducted as the basis for revising the BIP of a special education student. Three Basic Behavioral Intervention Plan forms are presented. They illustrate that there is more than one path to preparing a BIP, but all paths have common features.

The first form presents seven key questions to be answered by the teacher or the team:

> **What are the student's strengths?**
>
> **What are the problem behaviors?**
>
> **What do we want him/her to do?**
>
> **How will we teach the desired behaviors?**
>
> **What can he/she earn?**
>
> **What happens if he/she displays unacceptable behaviors?**
>
> **How long will we try this plan?**

Several actual examples of this approach are on the next pages, followed by brief comments and measurement considerations by the authors.

Example 1

Student's Name: _____*Anthony*_____ **Age:** _6_ **Grade:** _1_ **Date:** _____

What are his strengths?

Anthony is athletic. Peers like him because he is good in PE and playing physical games. He can do academic work well after receiving instruction .

What are the problem behaviors?

Anthony often comes to school late and misses important instruction. He becomes frustrated when he can't do the work. He crumples up his paper, taps his pencil, turns around in his chair and often escalates to the point where he has to be removed from class and sent to the office.

What do we want him to do?

Anthony needs to come to school on time. When he does come in late, he needs strategies to keep from getting frustrated and escalating. When he comes in late and doesn't know how to do a task he needs to calmly ask the teacher to explain the missed parts of the instruction.

How will we teach the desired behaviors?

Role-play what he needs to do when he comes in late.
Agree what he needs to do to minimize frustration:
1. Sharpen pencil when school is out so it is ready for the next day.
2. His lunch count ticket will be in a separate spot so he can fill it out quietly when he comes in late.
3. When he gets to parts in his work where he missed instruction, he will say to the teacher: "I missed that part, can you explain it to me?"

What can he earn?

Anthony can pick a game for the class to play during PE.
He can be a guide for a blind peer in class who loves to do physical activity.

What happens if he displays unacceptable behaviors?
Anthony will go to the office for time-out.

How long will we try this plan?
The plan will be tried for one week. Changes will be made as necessary.

Authors' Comments:

Anthony's strengths in PE provide direction in selecting his reinforcement. Since the planner is helping Anthony cope with being late, rather than working solely on eliminating the lateness, we should assume some of the tardiness is beyond Anthony's control.

Measurement Considerations:

1. One could count the number of times Anthony is sent to the office for unacceptable behaviors. The chart might be a spaceship attempting to land and stay safely on the runway (a zero occurrence rate).

2. One could count the number of times Anthony uses acceptable behaviors after being late. This, however, limits progress to the number of times he is late, and that is not desirable.

3. A combined count of "on times" plus acceptable behaviors when late might be a useful "positive" measure.

Example 2

Student's Name: _____ *Vanja* _____ **Age:** _11_ **Grade:** _5_ **Date:** _____

What are his strengths?

Vanja is academically above average. He has well developed, above average expressive language skills. He invents and writes interesting and great stories.

What are the problem behaviors?

Vanja acts out behind the teacher's back to get attention from peers.
He dances in place making suggestive sexual motions. He makes faces and inappropriate hand gestures.

What do we want him to do?

Vanja needs to act maturely, stay focused on his work and interact appropriately with his peers.

How will we teach the desired behaviors?

The teacher will talk to Vanja about what acting mature means and why it is important. He will role-play acceptable and unacceptable ways to get peer attention. Since Vanja likes peer attention, Mika, a mature peer whom Vanja likes a lot, will give Vanja feedback on his behavior by putting his thumb up or down throughout the day.

What can he earn?

Vanja will earn pluses or minuses on a daily chart. At the end of the day he can earn a "good day" star. When he has earned 3 stars, Vanja, Mika and an adult go to Dairy Queen for a treat.

What happens if he displays unacceptable behaviors?

Vanja will lose the privilege to be in class and go to an isolated area until the next period. If Vanja loses the privilege to be in class 3 times in one day, he will be in in-school suspension the next day where he will stay during recess and lunch and make up all missed work.

How long will we try this plan?

After one week, the team will meet to evaluate the plan and make changes if necessary.

Authors' Comments:

Peers such as Mika can sometimes be involved in positive, creative reinforcement as seen here. Mika provides "thumbs up" reinforcement to Vanja, and then both receive the Dairy Queen reinforcement.

Measurement Considerations:

1. The criteria for a "good day" star need to be spelled out and the dispenser of the pluses and minuses will need to have a clear plan, such as recording after each period, to ensure appropriate behaviors are not neglected and only minuses recorded.

2. The combination of recording pluses and minuses is analogous to an excellent practice in teaching reading in which both words read correctly per minute (in oral reading) and number of errors per minute are recorded on the same chart. In both cases, we hope to see the correct or acceptable numbers increase while the incorrect or error numbers decrease.

Example 3

Student's Name: _____ *Scott* _____ **Age:** _6_ **Grade:** _1_ **Date:** _____

What are his strengths?
Scott is very active, curious and athletic. He loves to play on the climbing structure on the playground.

What are the problem behaviors?
When Scott has difficulty performing an academic task, he throws things, tears up his paper and sulks.

What do we want him to do?
Scott needs to let the teacher know calmly that he has a difficult time doing the task.

How will we teach the desired behaviors?
Role-play with Scott how to ask for help before getting upset. The teacher will try to get additional help for Scott to improve his reading and math skills.

What can he earn?
Scott can earn extra recess time each day for staying calm.

What happens if he displays unacceptable behaviors?
If Scott is disruptive, he goes to a quiet place with an easier academic task. If he is still disruptive, Scott makes up wasted time during a preferred activity like recess.

How long will we try this plan?
The team will meet after 5 school days and adjust the plan if necessary.

Authors' Comments:

Again, a strength is the basis for Scott's reinforcement. It's important to note that the planners believe its effectiveness will be evident within a week. If the plan does not succeed as hoped, the team might examine and question the practice of using a quiet place with easier work as a consequence for unacceptable behavior. The plan could also specify that the teacher will make reasonable effort to insure that Scott is given only work he can do.

Measurement Considerations:

The easy observation here is that Scott could fake difficulty, remain calm and get extra recess. However, the alert teacher will insure that completing the academic task successfully is also reinforced. It's also unlikely that a first grader would be prone to faking. Nevertheless, it's a good idea, here as always, to monitor the plan closely and be prepared to adjust if necessary.

Example 4

Student's Name: _____*Ann*_____ **Age:** _14_ **Grade:** _8_ **Date:** _____

What are her strengths?
Ann designs outrageous outfits. She is very artistic.

What are the problem behaviors?
Ann draws graffiti on her desks, the walls in the hallways and in restrooms.

What do we want her to do?
Ann needs to draw only in appropriate places.

How will we teach the desired behaviors?
Talk to Ann and problem solve ways she can be creative without destroying property. With the help of the shop teacher, she can design graffiti boards for the classrooms and hallways. She can help plan ways that she and other students can earn opportunities to draw on the graffiti boards. Each day, Ann can check the boards, take off the paper and file preferred art or graffiti in a special notebook to be displayed publicly.

What can she earn?
Ann can earn time, opportunities to draw, and the privilege of managing the graffiti boards.

What happens if she displays unacceptable behaviors?
Ann will pay restitution and clean up graffiti, the cafeteria and the school grounds.

How long will we try this plan?
Two weeks.

Authors' Comments:

A trial of two weeks will, in all probability, be sufficient to determine the effectiveness of this plan. If a major drop in inappropriate placement of graffiti doesn't occur very quickly with this plan, it isn't likely to occur.

Measurement Considerations:

The frequency of inappropriate placement of graffiti seems the best measure to use here. Not only is it more efficient, but if one counted only appropriate placements, they could increase while there was no decrease at all in the problem behavior (inappropriate placement of graffiti).

Example 5

Student's Name: _____Luke_____ **Age:** _16_ **Grade:** _11_ **Date:**_____

What are his strengths?
Luke is very social and generous.

What are the problem behaviors?
Luke consistently misses the first two periods of each day (ten classes each week).

What do we want him to do?
Luke needs to attend all his classes consistently so he doesn't miss instruction and practice.

How will we teach the desired behaviors?
Problem solve with Luke. Suggest that for every four days he is in every class on time, he can earn a pass to have free time during one class period.

What can he earn?
He can earn free time.

What happens if he displays unacceptable behaviors?
Luke will need to come to Saturday school to make up any instruction missed because of the unacceptable behaviors.

How long will we try this plan?
After 10 school days, the team will meet to adjust the plan if necessary.

Authors' Comments:

This plan illustrates how the positive reinforcement (free time) and negative consequence (extra time in school) work in tandem, a powerful combination. A plan like this also deflates the power struggle that is likely taking place.

Measurement Considerations:

Clearly, classes attended or skipped could be counted and recorded. We hope and believe there will be fewer skipped classes, so it would be easier to track them.

Example 6

Student's Name: _____ *TJ* _____ **Age:** _5_ **Grade:** *Kdg* **Date:** _____

What are his strengths?

TJ likes to play on the computer and play video games. He likes to tell stories about his dad who is a truck driver.

What are the problem behaviors?

TJ often refuses to do work or follow directions. He hurts other children or himself.

What do we want him to do?

TJ needs to follow directions, complete assigned tasks and refrain from hurting others or himself.

How will we teach the desired behaviors?

Explain to TJ that he can earn computer time if he follows directions, does his work and uses his hands appropriately. Show him a chart with boxes for happy faces. Every 15 minutes he can earn a happy face. Teach TJ how to go to time-out if he doesn't follow directions.

What can he earn?

He can earn happy faces, computer time, and when his dad is in town, he can earn the privilege to call him at lunch time.

What happens if he displays unacceptable behaviors?

He will be asked to go to time-out.

How long will we try this plan?

The teacher will keep data on TJ's behavior and try the plan for a week.

Authors' Comments:

Once again, the reinforcers are carefully tailored to the child's strengths and interests. This is an important factor in developing successful BIPs. The one-size-fits-all approach to reinforcers is not nearly as effective as the individualized approach.

Measurement Considerations:

Counting the times TJ has to go to time-out for inappropriate behavior would be the most efficient record to keep. It is also possible to keep track of happy faces, computer time and phone calls. To do so would not be burdensome if TJ could manage self-charting. Whenever feasible, self-charting is a good idea, and has been shown to be effective.

Example 7

Student's Name: _____*Paul*_____ **Age:** *10* **Grade:** *4* **Date:** _____

What are his strengths?

Paul lives with his grandpa and likes to go fishing with him. Paul likes to work on mechanical things (e.g., toy car, bike, radio, engines) and he enjoys remote control cars and playing games on the computer. He is a great skateboarder and bike rider. He likes to do things for others.

What are the problem behaviors?

Paul gets into power struggles with his teacher and becomes non-compliant. When the teacher tells him what to do, he says things like, "You can't tell me what to do. F… you." "I'm not gonna do it. You can't make me. You F..B…"

What do we want him to do?

Paul needs to follow directions without getting upset. He needs to use appropriate language when talking to his teacher.

How will we teach the desired behaviors?

Discuss the importance of being respectful and following directions with Paul. Role-play appropriate and unacceptable behavior. Explain to Paul that he can earn pennies in a jar for respectfully following directions.

What can he earn?

With the pennies he can buy items from a menu of items (e.g., fishing time with grandpa, remote control car, computer time).

What happens if he displays unacceptable behaviors?

Paul will be asked to go to time-out and make up all wasted time during a preferred activity.

How long will we try this plan?

Two weeks.

Authors' Comments:

Paul is fortunate to have a teacher who treats his inappropriate language as a signal for teaching him more appropriate ways. Few teachers are so understanding. We all need to remind ourselves that teaching acceptable behaviors is far better than assuming the child knows how to perform them but is choosing not to do so. And we need to know not to personalize even wildly inappropriate outbursts.

Measurement Considerations:

Pennies earned could be the unit of measurement. However, in a well-managed plan, Paul will begin to receive additional reinforcement (teacher smiles and peer approval) for appropriate behavior, so greater periods of good behavior will be required. Therefore, perhaps counting hours with no problematic times would be better.

Example 8

Student's Name: _____ *Melissa* _____ **Age:** *12* **Grade:** *7* **Date:** _____

What are her strengths?

Melissa is a great runner. She likes to take care of young children.

What are the problem behaviors?

At unpredictable times during academic instruction, Melissa slouches in her chair and her inappropriate behaviors escalate. She throws books, pencils and furniture and yells profanities.

What do we want her to do?

As soon as Melissa starts to slouch in her chair, she needs to calm herself down to keep from escalating.

How will we teach the desired behaviors?

The teacher will make a large poster which says, " I am calm and good at what I do." When Melissa is calm, the teacher will teach Melissa with discussion and role-play. When Melissa slouches in her chair, the teacher will ask her to look at the sign and say to herself, "I am calm and good at what I do." She will repeat this until she has calmed herself down.

What can she earn?

If Melissa can calm herself down without being destructive, she earns the privilege to go to the kindergarten classroom and read stories to the kindergartners for 30 minutes.

What happens if she displays unacceptable behaviors?

The rest of the class will leave the classroom for a room clear. An assistant will stay in the room to supervise Melissa but will not interact with her at all until she has calmed down. Melissa will make up all wasted time during a preferred activity.

How long will we try this plan?

The teacher will keep track of each instance of escalating behaviors and evaluate the plan after 2 weeks.

Authors' Comments:

Melissa's unacceptable behaviors can pose a real danger to the other students. Therefore, the rather extreme measure of clearing all students from the room is justified.

Measurement Considerations:

Room clearings are going to be infrequent, we presume, and therefore easy to track. Remember that tracking a negative behavior does not mean that we are attending to it more than we should. Positive attention goes to acceptable behaviors, not to challenging behaviors. Record keeping can be separated from direct reinforcement of students.

Example 9

Student's Name: _____*Joey*_____ **Age:** _7_ **Grade:** _2_ **Date:** _____

What are his strengths?

Joey is athletic and has a well developed vocabulary. He loves adult attention and getting "stuff."

What are the problem behaviors?

Joey is sneaky. He takes things from other kids and from his parents.

What do we want him to do?

Joey needs to respect other people's property and ask for items that he wants.

How will we teach the desired behaviors?

The principal will talk to Joey and tell him that it is unacceptable to take things without asking. Joey's backpack and pockets will be checked each morning when he arrives and each afternoon before he goes home. If Joey sees an item he wants, he can come to the principal and tell him about the item.

What can he earn?

Joey can earn selected items he asks for and/or time for playing computer games in the principal's office.

What happens if he displays unacceptable behaviors?

If Joey takes things without asking, he needs to pay restitution by doing chores. He will scrub the breezeway wall with a brush and soap. Each 15 minutes cleaning segment will be worth $1.00.

How long will we try this plan?

Instances of reported stealing will be recorded. Depending on the increase or decrease of the instances, the plan will be reviewed and adjusted after one week.

Authors' Comments:

Before searching a child's backpack and pockets regularly, it would be wise to check with the school attorney and be sure the child and his parents are aware that these are areas where privacy is not expected under this plan. In some states, it might also be important to use Monopoly money, not real money, to pay restitution. In all cases, parent knowledge and approval of a behavior plan is critical.

Measurement Considerations:

The BIP itself specifies that instances of reported stealing will be recorded. That is appropriate in this situation.

Example 10

Student's Name: _____ *Meagan* _____ **Age:** _8_ **Grade:** _3_ **Date:** _____

What are her strengths?

Meagan loves to help people and animals. She has a great sense of humor.

What are the problem behaviors?

Meagan falls on the floor with her arm rigid and her eyes fluttering.
She produces fake seizures to get adult attention. Her brother with autism has real
seizures and Meagan imitates them when tasks are challenging or boring.
She has had all necessary medical exams, and this plan has been heartily
approved by her pediatrician and pediatric neurologist.

What do we want her to do?

Meagan needs to get adult attention in appropriate ways.

How will we teach the desired behaviors?

Meagan will be told that it is unacceptable to have seizures in school and will be taught,
by modeling and role-playing, how she can appropriately obtain adult attention.

What can she earn?

Meagan can earn the privilege of helping the teacher clean the rat cage and having the
pet rat on her desk during independent seat work, based on time with no seizures.

What happens if she displays unacceptable behaviors?

The teacher will do a room clear and ignore Meagan's "seizure" behavior. The janitor will
come in the room to supervise Meagan while pretending to be cleaning the blinds.
The janitor will not interact with Meagan.

How long will we try this plan?

The teacher will keep track of the number of times Meagan fakes a seizure and reevaluate
the plan after 2 weeks.

Authors' Comments:

The concept of faked seizures is not familiar to all of us, but they do indeed occur. There are even cases where the frequency of seizures has been reduced by withholding all reinforcers when they occur, without regard to a determination of the "genuineness" of the seizures.

Measurement Considerations:

The number of seizures is the unit and the goal is zero. Would that all measurement was so straight forward.

Example 11

Student's Name: _____ *Omar* _____ **Age:** _9_ **Grade:** _4_ **Date:** _____

What are his strengths?

Omar is very positive and friendly. He tries hard to please adults.
He loves snacks, trinkets, and other "stuff."

What are the problem behaviors?

Omar talks out in class. He blurts things out impulsively and interrupts
the teacher frequently.

What do we want him to do?

Omar needs to raise his hand in class to get permission to talk.

How will we teach the desired behaviors?

The teacher will role-play with Omar how to raise his hand appropriately.
The teacher will demonstrate the acceptable and unacceptable ways of asking for
permission to talk.

What can he earn?

Omar can earn a star each time he raises his hand quietly at an appropriate time.
When he has earned 20 stars, he can choose a trinket from the treasure box.

What happens if he displays unacceptable behaviors?

The teacher will not pay attention to Omar when he talks out or interrupts.

How long will we try this plan?

The teacher will keep track of Omar's talk-outs and when he quietly raises his hand.
The plan will be evaluated after one week.

Authors's Comments:

This is a common problem and a strikingly simple plan. The critical ingredient is the role-playing to teach Omar how to perform the acceptable behavior. Too often it is just assumed the child knows how to perform acceptably and is choosing not to do so.

Measurement Considerations:

Tracking both talk-outs and hand-raises is appropriate. We hope to see a data chart in which number of hand-raises goes up and number of talk-outs decreases to zero and stays there.

Example 12

Student's Name: _____ *Domingo* _____ **Age:** _13_ **Grade** _7_ **Date:** _____

What are his strengths?

Domingo has outstanding computer programming skills.
He develops computer games.

What are the problem behaviors?

Domingo bullies other students in the locker area during transition times. He pushes them up against the lockers and threatens to hurt them. He takes items from other students and destroys them.

What do we want him to do?

Domingo needs to keep his hands to himself, not bother other students and not destroy others' property.

How will we teach the desired behaviors?

The counselor will talk to Domingo about the importance of respecting others and their property. He will ask Domingo what can be done to keep him from bullying others. An adult will accompany Domingo during transitions between classes. All students in Domingo's class will be taught how to be properly assertive and how to deal with his bullying. Students will be asked to report any time they experience bullying by Domingo.

What can he earn?

During each transition, Domingo can earn 5 minutes of extra computer time.
The supervising adult will keep track of Domingo's behavior in the locker area.
The teacher will keep track of student reports on Domingo's behavior. Domingo can save up the time and use it to develop a game during school time.

What happens if he displays unacceptable behaviors?

Domingo will lose the privilege of access to any computer for a day.

How long will we try this plan?

The plan will be tried for 2 weeks.

Authors's Comments:

Again, the BIP is completely fitted to Domingo — his interests, his challenging behaviors and his rewards.

Measurement Considerations:

The extra computer time Domingo can earn seems to be a "natural," and chances are good (as they should be with every BIP) that the plan will be effective in a very short time. The more effective the plan, the less critical the measurement. Once we can say, "It's no longer a problem," our charts are not important (except perhaps, for research and sharing with others).

Example 13

Student's Name: _____*Rosita*_____ **Age:** *15* **Grade:** *9* **Date:** _____

What are her strengths?

Rosita is very attractive and popular. She is an excellent cook and loves to bake.

What are the problem behaviors?

During class time, Rosita writes notes and passes them to her friends.
She does not focus on the lesson but is trying to be social with her friends.

What do we want her to do?

Follow directions and pay attention in class.

How will we teach the desired behaviors?

Talk to her and emphasize the importance of paying attention in class.
Ask how that can occur. Role-play if necessary.

What can she earn?

Rosita can earn pluses or minuses for each period. After each period, the teacher will rate her with a plus or minus and record it. When Rosita has earned 10 pluses in a row, she may go to the home economics room and bake cookies for her class.

What happens if she displays unacceptable behaviors?

The teacher will confiscate the notes. During home economics,
Rosita will make up wasted time in the teacher's room.

How long will we try this plan?

The plan will be tried for 2 weeks.

Authors' Comments:

Once again, the positive reinforcer and the consequence for unacceptable behavior are two sides of the same coin — earning or forfeiting time in the home economics room.

Measurement Considerations:

Two measures are necessary here — a count of opportunities to go to the home economics room (10 pluses in a row) and minutes wasted while not earning a plus. Perhaps we can estimate the wasted minutes. The real world demands that we keep our data collection within the perspective of our first goal, which is to change behavior, be it academic, social or other.

Form Two

The information required on the next form is very similar to the information gathered for the last examples. If a functional behavior analysis is required, that data would be located in the top seven boxes while the behavior intervention plan is in the bottom four boxes. If, in a given situation, IDEA requires that an FBA be done, this form might be preferred simply because the essential components of a FBA, including the function (maintaining consequences) of the behavior, are more readily seen and more explicit than in the first form.

form 2

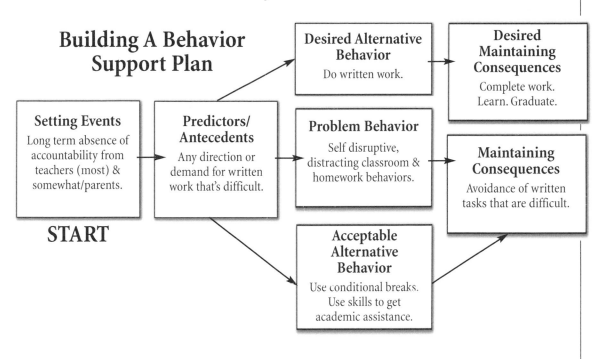

Building A Behavior Support Plan

Setting Events

Long term absence of accountability from teachers (most) & somewhat/parents.

START

Predictors/ Antecedents

Any direction or demand for written work that's difficult.

Desired Alternative Behavior

Do written work.

Desired Maintaining Consequences

Complete work. Learn. Graduate.

Problem Behavior

Self disruptive, distracting classroom & homework behaviors.

Maintaining Consequences

Avoidance of written tasks that are difficult.

Acceptable Alternative Behavior

Use conditional breaks. Use skills to get academic assistance.

Strategies/Action Plan

Changes in Setting Events

G. L. will only earn credit for completing the number of assignments required to pass a class.

Predictors/ Antecedents

Teachers will: provide opportunities to clarify written assignments for G.L. & to get assistance. Teachers will: negotiate appropriate break contingencies. Teachers will: reduce the length of assignments & break large assignments into smaller parts.

Replacement Behavior Skill Instruction

Teach the what, when & how of assignment clarification initiated by G. L. Teach when & how to take structured breaks. Practice keeping desk free of non-school materials.

Consequence Strategies

Begin use of tracker for monitoring classroom performance, following break procedure. Provide student with opportunities for regular & relevant feedback. Show students his progress visually with graph (bar or line).

(G.L. is a student who has a long history of refusing to do written work, failure to turn in assignments and disrupting the classroom when given written assignments. Form 2 illustrates a behavior support plan for G.L.)

Form Three

Some functional behavior analyses and behavior intervention plans are extraordinarily lengthy, filling many single-spaced pages. This level of complexity, detail, and sophistication may be required in a rare case. Our experience is that implementation of the Twenty Tips will reduce problem behavior in the classroom to a minimum. In those more difficult cases where the Twenty Tips are not sufficient when IDEA requires a special education student to have a written BIP and, perhaps, an FBA, we believe that the simplest form possible is usually best. Here is one more form, perhaps the simplest of all. Boxes 1 – 3 constitute a minimal FBA, and boxes 4 – 6 are the BIP.

The reader is invited to think of a particular student's problem behavior, past or present, and to complete this form in the order the boxes are numbered.

form 3

2 ← **1**   **3**

ANTECEDENT	TARGET BEHAVIOR	CONSEQUENCES

5 ← **4**   **6**

TEACHING PLAN	DESIRED BEHAVIOR	POSITIVE CONSEQUENCES

Final Words

Final Words

Teaching provides the opportunity to see children learn, mature, improve their social skills and so much more. The rewards can be huge, and every day (well, almost) can hold delightful moments when student behaviors are appropriate, respectful and pleasant. But if each day brings power struggles, acting out, disruption and disrespectful attitudes from students, the joys of teaching can be limited and hard to find.

For too many teachers, the biggest obstacle to developing a healthy classroom atmosphere is the belief that children willfully choose to misbehave, while knowing full well how to behave properly. Regardless of how often that may be true, there is a better way for teachers to think about student behaviors. Behavior is purposeful and behaviors that are repeated are those that accomplish a purpose — usually that of gaining attention or avoiding discomfort. Both purposes are absolutely basic and legitimate. The teacher's job is to provide a replacement behavior, an acceptable way for children to accomplish their purpose.

For a few teachers the deliberate use of positive reinforcement is a bit bothersome. The sense is that we shouldn't reward children for doing they are supposed to do, that students may only do the right thing when "bribed," or that they will just demand bigger and bigger rewards. Perhaps we need to step back and review the role of reinforcement in our own adult behavior to better appreciate the need for specific reinforcers for children learning new behaviors. The plain and simple fact is that we

do what's rewarding (reinforcing) and don't do what we find punishing (consequences). Millions of adults in this country have made an important and often difficult behavior change — quitting smoking. When one quits smoking, it's because **not smoking** has become more reinforcing than **smoking** — whether the reinforcers are a loved one's gratitude, better health, saving money or any other "m & m."

Many students, by the time they reach our classroom, are already hooked up to a reinforcement system — receiving powerful, intangible rewards for appropriate behavior — e.g., pride when work is completed, pleasure from the teacher's smile, peer acceptance, and satisfaction from an A or gold star or happy face. Many of the students with challenging behaviors aren't yet able to enjoy these reinforcers, so we meet them where they are and use tangible reinforcers. Just as in teaching academics, we must start at the student's level.

To sum it up:

1. Clearly teach your behavioral expectations;

2. Catch your students being good and make sure they know that you see and appreciate their appropriate behavior;

3. Implement any of the Twenty Tips you aren't already practicing; and

4. Enjoy your well-managed, positive classroom!

References

Sprague, J., Golly, A., Bernstein, L., March, R., & Munkres, A. (1999). *Building effective schools together (B.E.S.T.): A training guide for grades 1 – 12 translating research on effective schools into practice.* Eugene, OR: University of Oregon, Institute on Violence and Destructive Behavior.

Walker, H. M. (1995). *The acting-out child: Coping with classroom disruption* (2nd ed). Longmont, CO: Sopris West.

Walker, H. M., & Walker, J.E. (1991). *Coping with noncompliance in the classroom: A positive approach for teachers.* Austin, TX: Pro-Ed.

Walker, H. M., Stiller, B., Golly, A., Kavanagh, K., Severson, H., & Feil, E. (1997). *First step to success: Helping young children overcome antisocial behavior (an early intervention program for grades K – 3).* Longmont, CO: Sopris West.